A SERIES OF JESUS' POWERFUL WORDS

Whoever keeps Jesus' word will never see death.

(John 8, 51)

Book V

Jesus, the Miracle Maker

JESUS, THE MIRACLE MAKER

The signs of Jesus, His prayers, sermons, predictions and His appearances to His disciples after His triumphant resurrection are all contained in the gospels of Matthew, Mark, Luke and John and are enough for all those that hold doubts that Jesus was sent by God as Christ and Messiah to save this World

Prepared by

Peter Naumovich, Ph.D.

Naum Publishing

Grand Island, New York

Address all Inquires to the Publisher:
Naum Publishing
124 Colonial Drive
Grand Island, NY 14072
(716) 240 -7856

Editor: Peter Naumovich, Ph.D.
Technical Editor: Borka Naumovich, M.S.

This volume is published and printed in 2016
Copyright © 2016 by Naum Publishing
NPV20

Front cover: Icon of the Saviour, "Pantocrator", by Andrei
Erastov, 1992, with permission of the author. Illustrations: All illustrations in this book published in the
years 1875 through 1910.

Library of Congress Control Number: 2016910830

ISBN 978-0-9830926-4-3

Printed in the United States of America

PREFACE

Our Lord, Jesus Christ, once said: " ... *the word that you hear is not mine, but the Father's who sent me.*" (John 14, 24)

This Bible verse illustrates our only guideline: to compile all the words, thoughts and parables and extract and collect them so that they could be available and useful. All five books contain only verses of the New Testament, because it was only possible way to find these valuable and necessary thoughts and lessons.

Our Lord, Jesus Christ, by executing a task that the Father gave him left us as the most precious treasure of all: the Father's words and thoughts to help us in trouble, until his coming again.

To obtain a true picture of our Savior, his accomplishments and his triumphant resurrection, sometimes it is necessary, apart from the words of Jesus, to cite the thought and words of St. John the Baptist or the Apostles. These men were eye-witnesses of the events, all the humiliation and all suffering to which our Savior was exposed, all his short life.

These books consist of the words, thoughts, sayings and parables of our Lord Himself and they are accepted in all Christian churches.

Archaic Words

art = are

lo = look, see

thee = You
thine = Yours
thou = You
thy = Your

thou didst send = You sent
thou gavest = You have given
thou hast given = You have given
thou hast loved = You have loved
thou hast sent = You have sent
thou shouldst keep = You should keep
thou shouldst take = You should take
thou wilt = You want

Jesus did many other signs in the presence of the disciples, which are not written in this book; but these are written that you may believe that Jesus is the Christ, the Son of God, and that believing you may have life in his name. (John 20, 30. 31)

1. INTRODUCTION

The Baptism of Jesus

hen Jesus came from Galilee to the Jordan to John, to be baptized by him. John would have prevented him, saying:

♦ *I need to be baptized by you, and do you come to me?*

But Jesus answered him:

♦ *Let it be so now; for it is proper for us in this way to fulfill all righteousness.*

Then he consented. And when Jesus was baptized, he went up immediately from the water, and behold, the heavens were opened and he saw the Spirit of God descending like a dove, and alighting on him; and lo, a voice from heaven, saying:

♦ *This is my beloved Son, with whom I am well pleased.*

(Matthew 3, 13 - 17; Mark 1, 9 - 11; Luke 3, 21.22)

The First Disciples of Jesus

he next day again John was standing with two of his disciples; and he looked at Jesus as he walked, and said:

♦ *Behold, the Lamb of God!*

The two disciples heard him say this, and they followed Jesus. Jesus turned, and saw them following, and said to them:

♦ *What do you seek?*

And they said to him:

♦ *Rabbi* (which means Teacher), *where are you staying?*

He said to them:

♦ *Come and see.*

They came and saw where he was staying; and they stayed with him that day, for it was about the tenth hour. One of the two who heard John speak, and followed him, was Andrew, Simon Peter's brother. He first found his brother Simon, and said to him:

♦ *We have found the Messiah* (which means Christ).

He brought him to Jesus. Jesus looked at him, and said:

♦ *So you are Simon the son of John? You shall be called Cephas* (which means Peter).

(John 1, 35 - 42)

The Angels of God Ascending and Descending Upon the Son of Man

he next day Jesus decided to go to Galilee. And he found Philip and said to him:

♦ *Follow me.*

Now Philip was from Bethsaida, the city of Andrew and Peter. Philip

2

found Nathanael and said to him:

♦ *We have found him of whom Moses in the law and also the prophets wrote, Jesus of Nazareth, the son of Joseph.*

Nathanael said to him:

♦ *Can anything good come out of Nazareth?*

Philip said to him:

♦ *Come and see.*

Jesus saw Nathanael coming to him, and said of him:

♦ *Behold, an Israelite indeed, in whom is no guile!*

Nathanael said to him:

♦ *How do you know me?*

Jesus answered him:

♦ *Before Philip called you, when you were under the fig tree, I saw you.*

Nathanael answered him:

♦ *Rabbi, you are the Son of God! You are the King of Israel!*

Jesus answered him:

♦ *Because I said to you, I saw you under the fig tree, do you believe? You shall see greater things than these.*

And he said to him:

♦ *Truly, truly, I say to you, you will see heaven opened, and the an-*

3

angels of God ascending and descending upon the Son of man.

(John 1, 43 - 51)

2. THE SIGNS OF JESUS BEFORE THE FIRST PASSOVER

2.1 In Galilee

The Weddings in Cana

n the third day there was a marriage at Cana in Galilee, and the mother of Jesus was there; Jesus also was invited to the marriage, with his disciples. When the wine failed, the mother of Jesus said to him:

♦ *They have no wine.*

And Jesus said to her:

♦ *O woman, what have you to do with me? My hour has not yet come.*

His mother said to the servants:

♦ *Do whatever he tells you.*

Now six stone jars were standing there, for the Jewish rites of purification, each holding twenty or thirty gallons. Jesus said to them:

♦ *Fill the jars with water.*

And they filled them up to the brim. He said to them:

♦ *Now draw some out, and take it to the steward of the feast.*

So they took it. When the steward of the feast tasted the water now become wine, and did not know where it came from (though the servants who had drawn the water knew), the steward of the feast called the bridegroom and said to him:

♦ *Every man serves the good wine first; and when men have drunk freely, then the poor wine; but you have kept the good wine until now.*

This, the first of his signs, Jesus did at Cana in Galilee, and manifested his glory; and his disciples believed in him.

(John 2, 1 – 11)

3. THE SIGNS OF JESUS BETWEEN THE FIRST AND SECOND PASSOVER

3.1 *In Judea*

In Three Days the Temple Will Be Raised Up

he Jews then said to him:

♦ *What sign have you to show us for doing this?*

Jesus answered them:

♦ *Destroy this temple, and in three days I will raise it up.*

The Jews then said:

♦ *It has taken forty-six years to build this temple, and will you raise it up in three days?*

But he spoke of the temple of his body. When therefore he was raised from the dead, his disciples remembered that he had said this; and they believed the scripture and the word which Jesus had spoken.

(John 2, 18 - 22)

Jesus Teaches Nicodemus

hen he was in Jerusalem at the Passover feast, many believed in his name when they saw the signs which he did; but Jesus did not trust himself to them, because he knew all men and needed no one to bear witness of man; for he himself knew what was in man. Now there was a man of the Pharisees, named Nicodemus, a ruler of the Jews. This man came to Jesus by night and said to him:

♦ *Rabbi, we know that you are a teacher come from God; for no one can do these signs that you do, unless God is with him.*

Jesus answered him:

♦ *Truly, truly, I say to you, unless one is born anew, he cannot see the kingdom of God.*

Nicodemus said to him:

♦ *How can a man be born when he is old? Can he enter a second time into his mother's womb and be born?*

Jesus answered:

♦ *Truly, truly, I say to you, unless one is born of water and the Spirit, he cannot enter the kingdom of God. That which is born of the flesh is flesh, and that which is born of the Spirit is spirit. Do marvel that I said to you, `You must be born anew.'The wind blows where it wills, and you hear the sound of it, but you do not know whence it comes or whither it goes; so it is with every one who is born of the Spirit.*

6

Nicodemus said to him:

♦ *How can this be?*

Jesus answered him:

♦ *Are you a teacher of Israel, and yet you do not understand this?*

Truly, truly, I say to you, we speak of what we know, and bear witness to what we have seen; but you do not receive our testimony. If I have told you earthly things and you do not believe, how can you believe if I tell you heavenly things?

No one has ascended into heaven but he who descended from heaven, the Son of man. And as Moses lifted up the serpent in the wilderness, so must the Son of man be lifted up, that whoever believes in him may have eternal life.

For God so loved the world that he gave his only Son, that whoever believes in him should not perish but have eternal life.

For God sent the Son into the world, not to condemn the world, but that the world might be saved through him. He who believes in him is not condemned; he who does not believe is condemned already, because he has not believed in the name of the only Son of God.

And this is the judgment, that the light has come into the world, and men loved darkness rather than light, because their deeds were evil. For every one who does evil hates the light, and does not come to the light, lest his deeds should be exposed.

But he who does what is true comes to the light, that it may be clearly seen that his deeds have been wrought in God.

(John 2, 23 – 25; 3, 1 - 21)

7

3.2 *In Samaria*

Jesus Talks with a Samaritian Women

e left Judea and departed again to Galilee. He had to pass through Samaria. So he came to a city of Samaria, called Sychar, near the field that Jacob gave to his son Joseph. Jacob's well was there, and so Jesus, wearied as he was with his journey, sat down beside the well. It was about the sixth hour. There came a woman of Samaria to draw water. Jesus said to her:

♦ *Give me a drink.*

For his disciples had gone away into the city to buy food. The Samaritan woman said to him:

♦ *How is it that you, a Jew, ask a drink of me, a woman of Samaria?*

For Jews have no dealings with Samaritans. Jesus answered her:

♦ *If you knew the gift of God, and who it is that is saying to you, 'Give me a drink,' you would have asked him, and he would have given you living water.*

The woman said to him:

♦ *Sir, you have nothing to draw with, and the well is deep; where do you get that living water? Are you greater than our father Jacob, who gave us the well, and drank from it himself, and his sons, and his cattle?*

Jesus said to her:

♦ *Every one who drinks of this water will thirst again, but whoever drinks of the water that I shall give him will never thirst; the water that I shall give him will become in him a spring of water wel-*

ling up to eternal life.

The woman said to him:

♦ *Sir, give me this water, that I may not thirst, nor come here to draw.*

Jesus said to her:

♦ *Go, call your husband, and come here.*

The woman answered him:

♦ *I have no husband.*

Jesus said to her:

♦ *You are right in saying, `I have no husband'; for you have had five husbands, and he whom you now have is not your husband; this you said truly.*

The woman said to him:

♦ *Sir, I perceive that you are a prophet. Our fathers worshiped on this mountain; and you say that in Jerusalem is the place where men ought to worship.*

Jesus said to her:

♦ *Woman, believe me, the hour is coming when neither on this mountain nor in Jerusalem will you worship the Father. You worship what you do not know; we worship what we know, for salvation is from the Jews. But the hour is coming, and now is, when the true worshipers will worship the Father in spirit and truth, for such the Father seeks to worship him. God is spirit, and those who worship him must worship in spirit and truth."*

The woman said to him:

♦ *I know that Messiah is coming (he who is called Christ); when he comes, he will show us all things.*

Jesus said to her:

♦ *I who speak to you am he.*

♦ *Just then his disciples came. They marveled that he was talking with a woman, but none said, "What do you wish?" or, "Why are you talking with her?"*

So the woman left her water jar, and went away into the city, and said to the people:

♦ *Come, see a man who told me all that I ever did. Can this be the Christ?*

(John 4, 3 – 29)

3.3 *In Galilee*

Jesus Heals an Official's Son

o he came again to Cana in Galilee, where he had made the water wine. And at Capernaum there was an official whose son was ill. When he heard that Jesus had come from Judea to Galilee, he went and begged him to come down and heal his son, for he was at the point of death. Jesus therefore said to him:

♦ *Unless you see signs and wonders you will not believe.*

The official said to him:

♦ *Sir, come down before my child dies.*

Jesus said to him:

♦ *Go; your son will live.*

The man believed the word that Jesus spoke to him and went his way. As he was going down, his servants met him and told him that his son was living. So he asked them the hour when he began to mend, and they said to him:

♦ *Yesterday at the seventh hour the fever left him.*

The father knew that was the hour when Jesus had said to him:

♦ *Your son will live.*

And he himself believed, and all his household. This was now the second sign that Jesus did when he had come from Judea to Galilee.

(John 4, 46 – 54)

Jesus Heals a Man with an Evil Spirit

nd immediately there was in their synagogue a man with an unclean spirit; and he cried out:

♦ *What have you to do with us, Jesus of Nazareth? Have you come to destroy us? I know who you are, the Holy One of God.*

But Jesus rebuked him, saying:

♦ *Be silent, and come out of him!*

And the unclean spirit, convulsing him and crying with a loud voice, came out of him. And they were all amazed, so that they questioned among themselves, saying:

♦ *What is this? A new teaching! With authority he commands even*

11

the unclean spirits, and they obey him.

And at once his fame spread everywhere throughout all the surrounding region of Galilee.

(Mark 1, 23 – 28; Luke 4, 33 - 37)

Jesus Heals a Man with Leprosy

nd a leper came to him beseeching him, and kneeling said to him:

♦ *If you will, you can make me clean.*

Moved with pity, he stretched out his hand and touched him, and said to him:

♦ *I will; be clean.*

And immediately the leprosy left him, and he was made clean. And he sternly charged him, and sent him away at once, and said to him:

♦ *See that you say nothing to any one; but go, show yourself to the priest, and offer for your cleansing what Moses commanded, for a proof to the people.*

But he went out and began to talk freely about it, and to spread the news, so that Jesus could no longer openly enter a town, but was out in the country; and people came to him from every quarter.

(Mark 1, 40 – 45; Matthew 8, 1 – 4, Luke 5, 12 - 16)

Jesus Calls the First Disciples

hile the people pressed upon him to hear the word of God, he was standing by the lake of Gennesaret. And he saw two boats by the lake; but the fishermen had gone out of them and were washing their nets. Getting into one of the boats, which was Simon's, he asked him to put out a little from the land. And he sat down and taught the people from the boat. And when he had ceased speaking, he said to Simon:

♦ *Put out into the deep and let down your nets for a catch.*

And Simon answered:

♦ *Master, we toiled all night and took nothing! But at your word I will let down the nets.*

And when they had done this, they enclosed a great shoal of fish; and as their nets were breaking, they beckoned to their partners in the other boat to come and help them. And they came and filled both the boats, so that they began to sink. But when Simon Peter saw it, he fell down at Jesus' knees, saying:

♦ *Depart from me, for I am a sinful man, O Lord.*

For he was astonished, and all that were with him, at the catch of fish which they had taken; and so also were James and John, sons of Zebedee, who were partners with Simon. And Jesus said to Simon:

♦ *Do not be afraid; henceforth you will be catching men.*

And when they had brought their boats to land, they left everything and followed him.

(Luke 5, 1 – 11; Matthew 4, 18 – 22, Mark 1, 16 – 20)

13

Jesus Heals a Paralyzed Man
in Capernaum

nd when he returned to Capernaum after some days, it was reported that he was at home. And many were gathered together, so that there was no longer room for them, not even about the door; and he was preaching the word to them. And they came, bringing to him a paralytic carried by four men. And when they could not get near him because of the crowd, they removed the roof above him; and when they had made an opening, they let down the pallet on which the paralytic lay. And when Jesus saw their faith, he said to the paralytic

♦ *My son, your sins are forgiven.*

Now some of the scribes were sitting there, questioning in their hearts:

♦ Why does this man speak thus? It is blasphemy! Who can forgive sins but God alone?

And immediately Jesus, perceiving in his spirit that they thus questioned within themselves, said to them:

♦ Why do you question thus in your hearts? Which is easier, to say to the paralytic, `Your sins are forgiven,' or to say, `Rise, take up your pallet and walk'? But that you may know that the Son of man has authority on earth to forgive sins...

he said to the paralytic:

♦ ... I say to you, rise, take up your pallet and go home.

And he rose, and immediately took up the pallet and went out before them all; so that they were all amazed and glorified God, saying:

14

♦ We never saw anything like this!

(Mark 2, 1 – 12; Matthew 9, 1 – 8; Luke 5, 18 – 26)

4. THE SIGNS OF JESUS BETWEEN THE SECOND AND THIRD PASSOVER

4.1 In Jerusalem

The Healing at the Pool on a Sabbath

fter this there was a feast of the Jews, and Jesus went up to Jerusalem. Now there is in Jerusalem by the Sheep Gate a pool, in Hebrew called Bethzatha, which has five porticoes. In these lay a multitude of invalids, blind, lame, paralyzed. One man was there, who had been ill for thirty-eight years. When Jesus saw him and knew that he had been lying there a long time, he said to him:

♦ *Do you want to be healed?*

The sick man answered him:

♦ *Sir, I have no man to put me into the pool when the water is troubled, and while I am going another steps down before me.*

Jesus said to him:

♦ *Rise, take up your pallet, and walk.*

And at once the man was healed, and he took up his pallet and walked. Now that day was the sabbath. So the Jews said to the man who was cured:

♦ *It is the sabbath, it is not lawful for you to carry your pallet.*

15

But he answered them:

♦ *The man who healed me said to me, `Take up your pallet, and walk.'*

They asked him:

♦ *Who is the man who said to you, `Take up your pallet, and walk'?*

Now the man who had been healed did not know who it was, for Jesus had withdrawn, as there was a crowd in the place. Afterward, Jesus found him in the temple, and said to him:

♦ *See, you are well! Sin no more, that nothing worse befall you.*

The man went away and told the Jews that it was Jesus who had healed him. And this was why the Jews persecuted Jesus, because he did this on the sabbath.

(John 5, 1 – 16)

Anyone Who Hears Jesus' Word and Believes Him Has Passed from Death to Life

he man went away and told the Jews that it was Jesus who had healed him. And this was why the Jews persecuted Jesus, because he did this on the sabbath.

But Jesus answered them:

♦ *My Father is working still, and I am working.*

This was why the Jews sought all the more to kill him, because he not only broke the sabbath but also called God his Father, making not only broke the sabbath but also called God his Father, making himself equal with God. Jesus said to them:

16

♦ *Truly, truly, I say to you, the Son can do nothing of his own accord, but only what he sees the Father doing; for whatever he does, that the Son does likewise. For the Father loves the Son, and shows him all that he himself is doing; and greater works than these will he show him, that you may marvel. For as the Father raises the dead and gives them life, so also the Son gives life to whom he will.*

The Father judges no one, but has given all judgment to the Son, that all may honor the Son, even as they honor the Father. He who does not honor the Son does not honor the Father who sent him.

Truly, truly, I say to you, he who hears my word and believes him who sent me, has eternal life; he does not come into judgment, but has passed from death to life.

Truly, truly, I say to you, the hour is coming, and now is, when the dead will hear the voice of the Son of God, and those who hear will live. For as the Father has life in himself, so he has granted the Son also to have life in himself, and has given him authority to execute judgment, because he is the Son of man. Do not marvel at this; for the hour is coming when all who are in the tombs will hear his voice and come forth, those who have done good, to the resurrection of life, and those who have done evil, to the resurrection of judgment.

I can do nothing on my own authority; as I hear, I judge; and my judgment is just, because I seek not my own will but the will of him who sent me. If I bear witness to myself, my testimony is not true; there is another who bears witness to me, and I know that the testimony which he bears to me is true. You sent to John, and he has borne witness to the truth. Not that the testimony which I receive is from man; but I say this that you may be saved. He was a burning and shining lamp, and you were willing to rejoice for a while in his light. But the testimony which I have is greater than that of John; for the works which the Father has granted me to accomplish, these very works which I am doing, bear me witness that the Fa-

ther has sent me. And the Father who sent me has himself borne witness to me. His voice you have never heard, his form you have never seen; and you do not have his word abiding in you, for you do not believe him whom he has sent.

You search the scriptures, because you think that in them you have eternal life; and it is they that bear witness to me; yet you refuse to come to me that you may have life.

I do not receive glory from men. But I know that you have not the love of God within you. I have come in my Father's name, and you do not receive me; if another comes in his own name, him you will receive. How can you believe, who receive glory from oneanother and do not seek the glory that comes from the only God?

Do not think that I shall accuse you to the Father; it is Moses who accuses you, on whom you set your hope. If you believed Moses, you would believe me, for he wrote of me. But if you do not believe his writings, how will you believe my words?

After this Jesus went to the other side of the Sea of Galilee, which is the Sea of Tiberias. And a multitude followed him, because they saw the signs which he did on those who were diseased.

(John 5, 15 – 47; 6, 1. 2)

The Son of Man, Greater Than the Temple, Is Lord of the Sabbath

A t that time Jesus went through the grainfields on the sabbath; his disciples were hungry, and they began to pluck heads of grain and to eat. But when the Pharisees saw it, they said to him:

♦ *Look, your disciples are doing what is not lawful to do on the sab-*

18

bath.

He said to them:

♦ *Have you not read what David did, when he was hungry, and those who were with him: how he entered the house of God and ate the bread of the Presence, which it was not lawful for him to eat nor for those who were with him, but only for the priests? Or have you not read in the law how on the sabbath the priests in the temple profane the sabbath, and are guiltless? I tell you, something greater than the temple is here. And if you had known what this means, `I desire mercy, and not sacrifice,' you would not have condemned the guiltless. For the Son of man is lord of the sabbath.*

(Matthew 12, 1 – 8, Mark 2, 23 – 24; Luke 6, 1 – 5)

Jesus Heals a Man with a Withered Hand

n another sabbath, when he entered the synagogue and taught, a man was there whose right hand was withered. And the scribes and the Pharisees watched him, to see whether he would heal on the sabbath, so that they might find an accusation against him. But he knew their thoughts, and he said to the man who had the withered hand:

♦ *Come and stand here.*

And he rose and stood there. And Jesus said to them:

♦ *I ask you, is it lawful on the sabbath to do good or to do harm, to save life or to destroy it?*

And he looked around on them all, and said to him:

♦ *Stretch out your hand.*

19

And he did so, and his hand was restored. But they were filled with fury and discussed with one another what they might do to Jesus.

(Luke 6, 6 – 11; Matthew 12, 9 – 14; Mark 3, 1 – 6)

4.2 *In Galilee and Around the Sea of Galilee*

The Sermon on the Mount

nd he (Jesus) went about all Galilee, teaching in their synagogues and preaching the gospel of the kingdom and healing every disease and every infirmity among the people. So his fame spread throughout all Syria, and they brought him all the sick, those afflicted with various diseases and pains,demoniacs, epileptics, and paralytics, and he healed them. And great crowds followed him from Galilee and the Decapolis and Jerusalem and Judea and from beyond the Jordan.

Seeing the crowds, he went up on the mountain, and when he sat down his disciples came to him. And he opened his mouth and taught them, saying:

♦ *Blessed are the poor in spirit, for theirs is the kingdom of heaven. Blessed are those who mourn, for they shall be comforted. Blessed are the meek, for they shall inherit the earth. Blessed are those who hunger and thirst for righteousness, for they shall be satisfied. Blessed are the merciful, for they shall obtain mercy. Blessed are the pure in heart, for they shall see God. Blessed are the peacemakers, for they shall be called sons of God. Blessed are those who are persecuted for righteousness' sake, for theirs is the kingdom of heaven. Blessed are you when men revile you and persecute you and utter all kinds of evil against you falsely on my account.*

Rejoice and be glad, for your reward is great in heaven, for so men persecuted the prophets who were before you.

20

You are the salt of the earth; but if salt has lost its taste, how shall its saltness be restored? It is no longer good for anything except to be thrown out and trodden under foot by men. You are the light of the world. A city set on a hill cannot be hid.

Nor do men light a lamp and put it under a bushel, but on a stand, and it gives light to all in the house. Let your light so shine before men, that they may see your good works and give glory to your Father who is in heaven.

Think not that I have come to abolish the law and the prophets; I have come not to abolish them but to fulfil them.

For truly, I say to you, till heaven and earth pass away, not an iota, not a dot, will pass from the law until all is accomplished. Whoever then relaxes one of the least of these commandments and teaches men so, shall be called least in the kingdom of heaven; but he who does them and teaches them shall be called great in the kingdom of heaven.

For I tell you, unless your righteousness exceeds that of the scribes and Pharisees, you will never enter the kingdom of heaven.

You have heard that it was said to the men of old, `You shall not kill; and whoever kills shall be liable to judgment.' But I say to you that every one who is angry with his brother shall be liable to judgment; whoever insults his brother shall be liable to the council, and whoever says, `You fool!' shall be liable to the hell of fire. So if you are offering your gift at the altar, and there remember that your brother has something against you, leave your gift there before the altar and go; first be reconciled to your brother, and then come and offer your gift. Make friends quickly with your accuser, while you are going with him to court, lest your accuser hand you over to the judge, and the judge to the guard, and you be put in prison; truly, I say to you, you will never get out till you have paid the last

21

penny.

*You have heard that it was said, `You shall not commit adultery.'
But I say to you that every one who looks at a woman lustfully has
already committed adultery with her in his heart. If your right eye
causes you to sin, pluck it out and throw it away; it is better that
you lose one of your members than that your whole body be thrown
into hell. And if your right hand causes you to sin, cut it off and
throw it away; it is better that you lose one of your members than
that your whole body go into hell. It was also said, `Whoever di-
vorces his wife, let him give her a certificate of divorce.' But I say
to you that every one who divorces his wife, except on the ground
of unchastity, makes her an adulteress; and whoever marries a di-
vorced woman commits adultery.*

*Again you have heard that it was said to the men of old, `You shall
not swear falsely, but shall perform to the Lord what you have sworn.'
But I say to you, Do not swear at all, either by heaven, for it is the
throne of God, or by the earth, for it is his footstool, or by Jerusalem, for it is the city of the great King. And do not swear by your
head, for you cannot make one hair white or black. Let what you
say be simply `Yes' or `No'; anything more than this comes from
evil.*

*You have heard that it was said, `An eye for an eye and a tooth
for a tooth.' But I say to you, Do not resist one who is evil. But
if any one strikes you on the right cheek, turn to him the other also;
and if any one would sue you and take your coat, let him have
your cloak as well; and if any one forces you to go one mile, go
with him two miles. Give to him who begs from you, and do not
refuse him who would borrow from you.*

*You have heard that it was said, `You shall love your neighbor and
hate your enemy.' But I say to you, Love your enemies and pray for
those who persecute you, so that you may be sons of your Father*

who is in heaven; for he makes his sun rise on the evil and on the good, and sends rain on the just and on the unjust. For if you love those who love you, what reward have you? Do not even the tax collectors do the same? And if you salute only your brethren, what more are you doing than others? Do not even the Gentiles do the same? You, therefore, must be perfect, as your heavenly Father is perfect.

Beware of practicing your piety before men in order to be seen by them; for then you will have no reward from your Father who is in heaven. Thus, when you give alms, sound no trumpet before you, as the hypocrites do in the synagogues and in the streets, that they may be praised by men. Truly, I say to you, they have received their reward. But when you give alms, do not let your left hand know what your right hand is doing, so that your alms may be in secret; and your Father who sees in secret will reward you. And when you pray, you must not be like the hypocrites; for they love to stand and pray in the synagogues and at the street corners, that they may be seen by men. Truly, I say to you, they have received their reward.

But when you pray, go into your room and shut the door and pray to your Father who is in secret; and your Father who sees in secret will reward you. And in praying do not heap up empty phrases as the Gentiles do; for they think that they will be heard for their many words. Do not be like them, for your Father knows what you need before you ask him. Pray then like this:

> *Our Father who art in heaven,*
> *Hallowed be thy name.*
> *Thy kingdom come.*
> *Thy will be done, On earth as it is in heaven.*
> *Give us this day our daily bread;*
> *And forgive us our debts,*
> *As we also have forgiven our debtors;*

23

And lead us not into temptation,
But deliver us from evil.

For if you forgive men their trespasses, your heavenly Father also will forgive you; but if you do not forgive men their trespasses, neither will your Father forgive your trespasses.

And when you fast, do not look dismal, like the hypocrites, for they disfigure their faces that their fasting may be seen by men. Truly, I say to you, they have received their reward. But when you fast, anoint your head and wash your face, that your fasting may not be seen by men but by your Father who is in secret; and your Father who sees in secret will reward you.

Do not lay up for yourselves treasures on earth, where moth and rust consume and where thieves break in and steal, but lay up for yourselves treasures in heaven, where neither moth nor rust consumes and where thieves do not break in and steal. For where your treasure is, there will your heart be also.

The eye is the lamp of the body. So, if your eye is sound, your whole body will be full of light; but if your eye is not sound, your whole body will be full of darkness. If then the light in you is darkness, how great is the darkness!

No one can serve two masters; for either he will hate the one and love the other, or he will be devoted to the one and despise the other. You cannot serve God and mammon. Therefore I tell you, do not be anxious about your life, what you shall eat or what you shall drink, nor about your body, what you shall put on. Is not life more than food, and the body more than clothing? Look at the birds of the air: they neither sow nor reap nor gather into barns, and yet your heavenly Father feeds them. Are you not of more value than they? And which of you by being anxious can add one cubit to his span of life? And why are you anxious about clothing? Consider

24

the lilies of the field, how they grow; they neither toil nor spin; yet I tell you, even Solomon in all his glory was not arrayed like one of these. But if God so clothes the grass of the field, which today is alive and tomorrow is thrown into the oven, will he not much more clothe you, O men of little faith? Therefore do not be anxious, saying, `What shall we eat?' or `What shall we drink?' or `What shall we wear?' For the Gentiles seek all these things; and your heavenly Father knows that you need them all. But seek first his kingdom and his righteousness, and all these things shall be yours as well.

Therefore do not be anxious about tomorrow, for tomorrow will be anxious for itself. Let the day's own trouble be sufficient for the day.

Judge not, that you be not judged. For with the judgment you pronounce you will be judged, and the measure you give will be the measure you get. Why do you see the speck that is in your brother's eye, but do not notice the log that is in your own eye? Or how can you say to your brother, `Let me take the speck out of your eye,' when there is the log in your own eye? You hypocrite, first take the log out of your own eye, and then you will see clearly to take the speck out of your brother's eye.

Do not give dogs what is holy; and do not throw your pearls before swine, lest they trample them under foot and turn to attack you.

Ask, and it will be given you; seek, and you will find; knock, and it will be opened to you. For every one who asks receives, and he who seeks finds, and to him who knocks it will be opened. Or what man of you, if his son asks him for bread, will give him a stone? Or if he asks for a fish, will give him a serpent? If you then, who are evil, know how to give good gifts to your children, how much more will your Father who is in heaven give good things to those who ask him!

25

So whatever you wish that men would do to you, do so to them; for this is the law and the prophets.

Enter by the narrow gate; for the gate is wide and the way is easy, that leads to destruction, and those who enter by it are many. For the gate is narrow and the way is hard, that leads to life, and those who find it are few.

Beware of false prophets, who come to you in sheep's clothing but inwardly are ravenous wolves. You will know them by their fruits. Are grapes gathered from thorns, or figs from thistles? So, every sound tree bears good fruit, but the bad tree bears evil fruit. A sound tree cannot bear evil fruit, nor can a bad tree bear good fruit. Every tree that does not bear good fruit is cut down and thrown into the fire. Thus you will know them by their fruits.

Not every one who says to me, `Lord, Lord,' shall enter the kingdom of heaven, but he who does the will of my Father who is in heaven. On that day many will say to me, `Lord, Lord, did we not prophesy in your name, and cast out demons in your name, and do many mighty works in your name?' And then will I declare to them, `I never knew you; depart from me, you evildoers.'

Every one then who hears these words of mine and does them will be like a wise man who built his house upon the rock; and the rain fell, and the floods came, and the winds blew and beat upon that house, but it did not fall, because it had been founded on the rock. And every one who hears these words of mine and does not do them will be like a foolish man who built his house upon the sand; and the rain fell, and the floods came, and the winds blew and beat against that house, and it fell; and great was the fall of it.

And when Jesus finished these sayings, the crowds were astonished at his teaching, for he taught them as one who had authority, and not as their scribes. When he came down from the mountain, great crowds followed him.

(Matthew 4, 23 - 25;   5, 1 – 48;   6, 1 – 34;   7, 1 – 29;   8, 1; Luke 6, 1 – 5)

Jesus Heals a Centurion's Servant

s he entered Capernaum, a centurion came forward to him, beseeching him and saying:

♦ *Lord, my servant is lying paralyzed at home, in terrible distress*

And he said to him:

♦ *I will come and heal him.*

But the centurion answered him:

♦ *Lord, I am not worthy to have you come under my roof; but only say the word, and my servant will be healed. For I am a man under authority, with soldiers under me; and I say to one, `Go,' and he goes, and to another, `Come,' and he comes, and to my slave, `Do this,' and he does it.*

When Jesus heard him, he marveled, and said to those who followed him:

♦ *Truly, I say to you, not even in Israel have I found such faith. I tell you, many will come from east and west and sit at table with Abraham, Isaac, and Jacob in the kingdom of heaven, while the sons of the kingdom will be thrown into the outer darkness; there men will weep and gnash their teeth.*

And to the centurion Jesus said:

27

♦ *Go; be it done for you as you have believed.*

And the servant was healed at that very moment.

(Matthew 8, 5 – 13; Luke 7, 1 – 10)

Jesus Raises a Widow's Son

 oon afterward he went to a city called Nain, and his disciples and a great crowd went with him. As he drew near to the gate of the city, behold, a man who had died was being carried out, the only son of his mother, and she was a widow; and a large crowd from the city was with her. And when the Lord saw her, he had compassion on her and said to her:

♦ *Do not weep.*

And he came and touched the bier, and the bearers stood still. And he said:

♦ *Young man, I say to you, arise.*

And the dead man sat up, and began to speak. And he gave him to his mother. Fear seized them all; and they glorified God, saying:

♦ *A great prophet has arisen among us!*

and

♦ *God has visited his people!*

(Luke 7, 11 – 16)

28

The Messengers from John the Baptist

ow when John heard in prison about the deeds of the Christ, he sent word by his disciples and said to him:

♦ *Are you he who is to come, or shall we look for another?*

And Jesus answered them:

♦ *Go and tell John what you hear and see: the blind receive their sight and the lame walk, lepers are cleansed and the deaf hear, and the dead are raised up, and the poor have good news preached to them. And blessed is he who takes no offense at me.*

(Matthew 11, 2 – 6;   Luke 17, 17 – 23)

Many Sins Have Been Forgiven by Those Who Have Shown Great Love

ne of the Pharisees asked him to eat with him, and he went into the Pharisee's house, and took his place at table. And behold, a woman of the city, who was a sinner, when she learned that he was at table in the Pharisee's house, brought an alabaster flask of ointment, and standing behind him at his feet, weeping, she began to wet his feet with her tears, and wiped them with the hair of her head, and kissed his feet, and anointed them with the ointment. Now when the Pharisee who had invited him saw it, he said to himself:

♦ *If this man were a prophet, he would have known who and what sort of woman this is who is touching him, for she is a sinner.*

And Jesus answering said to him:

♦ *Simon, I have something to say to you.*

29

And he answered:

♦ *What is it, Teacher?*

♦ *A certain creditor had two debtors; one owed five hundred denarii, and the other fifty. When they could not pay, he forgave them both. Now which of them will love him more?*

-Simon answered:

♦ *The one, I suppose, to whom he forgave more.*

And he said to him:

♦ *You have judged rightly.*

Then turning toward the woman, he said to Simon:

♦ *Do you see this woman? I entered your house, you gave me no water for my feet, but she has wet my feet with her tears and wiped them with her hair. You gave me no kiss, but from the time I came in she has not ceased to kiss my feet. You did not anoint my head with oil, but she has anointed my feet with ointment. Therefore I tell you, her sins, which are many, are forgiven, for she loved much; but he who is forgiven little, loves little.*

And he said to her:

♦ *Your sins are forgiven.*

Then those who were at table with him began to say among themselves:

♦ *Who is this, who even forgives sins?*

And he said to the woman:

♦ *Your faith has saved you; go in peace.*

(Luke 7, 36 – 50)

Jesus Calms a Storm

n that day, when evening had come, he said to them (to his disciples):

♦ *Let us go across to the other side.*

And leaving the crowd, they took him with them in the boat, just as he was. And other boats were with him. And a great storm of wind arose, and the waves beat into the boat, so that the boat was already filling.

But he was in the stern, asleep on the cushion; and they woke him and said to him:

♦ *Teacher, do you not care if we perish?*

And he awoke and rebuked the wind, and said to the sea:

♦ *Peace! Be still!*

And the wind ceased, and there was a great calm. He said to them:

♦ *Why are you afraid? Have you no faith?*

And they were filled with awe, and said to one another:

♦ *Who then is this, that even the wind and the sea obey him?*

(Mark 4, 35 – 41; Matthew 8, 23 – 27; Luke 8, 22 – 25)

Jesus Heals a Man with an Unclean Spirit

hey came (Jesus and disciples) to the other side of the sea, to the country of the Gerasenes. And when he had come out of the boat, there met him out of the tombs a man with an unclean spirit, who lived among the tombs; and no one could bind him any more, even with a chain; for he had often been bound with fetters and chains, but the chains he wrenched apart, and the fetters he broke in pieces; and no one had the strength to subdue him. Night and day among the tombs and on the mountains he was always crying out, and bruising himself with stones. And when he saw Jesus from afar, he ran and worshiped him; and crying out with a loud voice, he said:

♦ *What have you to do with me, Jesus, Son of the Most High God? I adjure you by God, do not torment me.*

For he had said to him:

♦ *Come out of the man, you unclean spirit!*

And Jesus asked him:

♦ *What is your name?*

He replied:

♦ *My name is Legion; for we are many.*

And he begged him eagerly not to send them out of the country. Now a great herd of swine was feeding there on the hillside; and they begged him:

♦ *Send us into the swine; let us enter them.*

So he gave them leave. And the unclean spirits came out, and entered the swine; and the herd, numbering about two thousand, rushed down the steep bank into the sea, and were drowned in the sea. The herdsmen fled, and told it in the city and in the country. And people came to see what it was that had happened. And they came to Jesus, and saw the demoniac sitting there, clothed and in his right mind, the man who had had the legion; and they were afraid. And those who had seen it told what had happened to the demoniac and to the swine. And they began to beg Jesus to depart from their neighborhood. And as he was getting into the boat, the man who had been possessed with demons begged him that he might be with him. But he refused, and said to him:

♦ *Go home to your friends, and tell them how much the Lord has done for you, and how he has had mercy on you.*

And he went away and began to proclaim in the Decapolis how much Jesus had done for him; and all men marveled.

(Mark 5, 1 – 20; Matthew 8, 28 – 34; Luke 8, 26 – 39)

Jesus Heals the Woman with Hemorrhages

nd a great crowd followed him and thronged about him. And there was a woman who had had a flow of blood for twelve years, and who had suffered much under many physicians, and had spent all that she had, and was no better but rather grew worse. She had heard the reports about Jesus, and came up behind him in the crowd and touched his garment. For she said:

♦ *If I touch even his garments, I shall be made well.*

And immediately the hemorrhage ceased; and she felt in her body that she was healed of her disease. And Jesus, perceiving in himself that power had gone forth from him, immediately turned about in the crowd, and said:

33

♦ *Who touched my garments?*

And his disciples said to him:

♦ *You see the crowd pressing around you, and yet you say, `Who touched me?*

And he looked around to see who had done it. But the woman, knowing what had been done to her, came in fear and trembling and fell down before him, and told him the whole truth. And he said to her:

♦ *Daughter, your faith has made you well; go in peace, and be healed of your disease.*

(Mark 5, 24 – 34; Matthew 9, 20 – 22; Luke 8, 43 – 48)

Jesus Raises Jairus' Daughter

nd when Jesus had crossed again in the boat to the other side, a great crowd gathered about him; and he was beside the sea. Then came one of the rulers of the synagogue, Jairus by name; and seeing him, he fell at his feet, and besought him, saying:

♦ *My little daughter is at the point of death. Come and lay your hands on her, so that she may be made well, and live.*

And he went with him. And a great crowd followed him and thronged about him. While he was still speaking, there came from the ruler's house some who said:

♦ *Your daughter is dead. Why trouble the Teacher any further?*

But ignoring what they said, Jesus said to the ruler of the synagogue:

♦ *Do not fear, only believe.*

And he allowed no one to follow him except Peter and James and John the brother of James. When they came to the house of the ruler of the synagogue, he saw a tumult, and people weeping and wailing loudly. And when he had entered, he said to them:

♦ *Why do you make a tumult and weep? The child is not dead but sleeping.*

And they laughed at him. But he put them all outside, and took the child's father and mother and those who were with him, and went in where the child was. Taking her by the hand he said to her:

♦ *Talitha cumi;*

which means:

♦ *Little girl, I say to you, arise.*

And immediately the girl got up and walked (she was twelve years of age), and they were immediately overcome with amazement. And he strictly charged them that no one should know this, and told them to give her something to eat.

(Mark 5, 21 – 24; 35 – 43; Matthew 9, 18. 19; 23 – 26; Luke 8, 40 – 42; 49 - 56)

Jesus Heals Two Blind Men

nd as Jesus passed on from there, two blind men followed him, crying aloud:

♦ *Have mercy on us, Son of David.*

When he entered the house, the blind men came to him; and Jesus said to them:

♦ *Do you believe that I am able to do this?*

They said to him:

♦ *Yes, Lord.*

Then he touched their eyes, saying:

♦ *According to your faith be it done to you.*

And their eyes were opened. Then Jesus sternly charged them:

♦ *See that no one knows it.*

But they went away and spread his fame through all that district.

(Matthew 9, 27 – 31)

Jesus Feeds Five Thousand Men

ow when Jesus heard this* he withdrew from there in a boat to a lonely place apart. But when the crowds heard it, they followed him on foot from the towns. As he went ashore he saw a great throng; and he had compassion on them, and healed their sick. When it was evening, the disciples came to him and said:

♦ *This is a lonely place, and the day is now over; send the crowds away to go into the villages and buy food for themselves.*

Jesus said:

♦ *They need not go away; you give them something to eat.*

They said to him:

36

♦ *We have only five loaves here and two fish.*

And he said:

♦ *Bring them here to me.*

Then he ordered the crowds to sit down on the grass; and taking the five loaves and the two fish he looked up to heaven, and blessed, and broke and gave the loaves to the disciples, and the disciples gave them to the crowds. And they all ate and were satisfied. And they took up twelve baskets full of the broken pieces left over. And those who ate were about five thousand men, besides women and children.

---

* that John the Baptist's disciples took his body and burred it

(Matthew 14, 13 - 21;   Mark 6, 30 – 44;   Luke 9, 10 – 17;   John 6, 3 – 13)

Jesus Walks on the Water

hen he made the disciples get into the boat and go before him to the other side, while he dismissed the crowds. And after he had dismissed the crowds, he went up on the mountain by himself to pray. When evening came, he was there alone, but the boat by this time was many furlongs distant from the land, beaten by the waves; for the wind was against them. And in the fourth watch of the night he came to them, walking on the sea. But when the disciples saw him walking on the sea, they were terrified, saying:

♦ *It is a ghost!*

And they cried out for fear. But immediately he spoke to them, saying:

♦ *Take heart, it is I; have no fear.*

And Peter answered him:

♦ *Lord, if it is you, bid me come to you on the water.*

He said:

♦ *Come.*

So Peter got out of the boat and walked on the water and came to Jesus; but when he saw the wind, he was afraid, and beginning to sink he cried out:

♦ *Lord, save me.*

Jesus immediately reached out his hand and caught him, saying to him:

♦ *O man of little faith, why did you doubt?*

And when they got into the boat, the wind ceased. And those in the boat worshiped him, saying:

♦ *Truly you are the Son of God.*

(Matthew 14, 22 - 33;   Mark 6, 45 – 51;   John 6, 15 – 21)

Jesus the Bread of Life

o when the people saw that Jesus was not there, nor his disciples, they themselves got into the boats and went to Capernaum, seeking Jesus. When they found him on the other side of the sea, they said to him:

♦ *Rabbi, when did you come here?*

Jesus answered them:

38

♦ *Truly, truly, I say to you, you seek me, not because you saw signs, but because you ate your fill of the loaves. Do not labor for the food which the Son of man will give to you; for on him has God the Father set his seal.*

Then they said to him:

♦ *What must we do, to be doing the works of God?*

Jesus answered them:

♦ *This is the work of God, that you believe in him whom he has sent.*

So they said to him:

♦ *Then what sign do you do, that we may see, and believe you? What work do you perform? Our fathers ate the manna in the wilderness; as it is written, `He gave them bread from heaven to eat.'*

Jesus then said to them:

♦ *Truly, truly, I say to you, it was not Moses who gave you the bread from heaven; my Father gives you the true bread from heaven. For the bread of God is that which comes down from heaven, and gives life to the world.*

They said to him:

♦ *Lord, give us this bread always.*

Jesus said to them:

♦ *I am the bread of life; he who comes to me shall not hunger, and he who believes in me shall never thirst. But I said to you that you have seen me and yet do not believe. All that the Father gives me will come to me; and him who comes to me I will not cast out. For I have come down from heaven, not to do my own will, but the will*

39

of him who sent me; and this is the will of him who sent me, that I should lose nothing of all that he has given me, but raise it up at the last day. For this is the will of my Father, that every one who sees the Son and believes in him should have eternal life; and I will raise him up at the last day.

The Jews then murmured at him, because he said:

♦ *I am the bread which came down from heaven.*

They said:

♦ *Is not this Jesus, the son of Joseph, whose father and mother we know? How does he now say, `I have come down from heaven'?*

Jesus answered them:

♦ *Do not murmur among yourselves. No one can come to me unless the Father who sent me draws him; and I will raise him up at the last day. It is written in the prophets, `And they shall all be taught by God.' Every one who has heard and learned from the Father comes to me. Not that any one has seen the Father except him who is from God; he has seen the Father. Truly, truly, I say to you, he who believes has eternal life. I am the bread of life. Your fathers ate the manna in the wilderness, and they died. This is the bread which comes down from heaven, that a man may eat of it and not die. I am the living bread which came down from heaven; if any one eats of this bread, he will live for ever; and the bread which I shall give for the life of the world is my flesh.*

The Jews then disputed among themselves, saying:

♦ *How can this man give us his flesh to eat?*

So Jesus said to them:

♦ *Truly, truly, I say to you, unless you eat the flesh of the Son of man*

40

and drink his blood, you have no life in you; he who eats my flesh and drinks my blood has eternal life, and I will raise him up at the last day. For my flesh is food indeed, and my blood is drink indeed. He who eats my flesh and drinks my blood abides in me, and I in him. As the living Father sent me, and I live because of the Father, so he who eats me will live because of me. This is the bread which came down from heaven, not such as the fathers ate and died; he who eats this bread will live for ever.

This he said in the synagogue, as he taught at Capernaum. Many of his disciples, when they heard it, said:

♦ *This is a hard saying; who can listen to it?*

But Jesus, knowing in himself that his disciples murmured at it, said to them:

♦ *Do you take offense at this? Then what if you were to see the Son of man ascending where he was before? It is the spirit that gives life, the flesh is of no avail; the words that I have spoken to you are spirit and life. But there are some of you that do not believe.*

For Jesus knew from the first who those were that did not believe, and who it was that would betray him. And he said:

♦ *This is why I told you that no one can come to me unless it is granted him by the Father.*

After this many of his disciples drew back and no longer went about with him. Jesus said to the twelve:

♦ *Do you also wish to go away?*

Simon Peter answered him:

♦ *Lord, to whom shall we go? You have the words of eternal life; and*

41

we have believed, and have come to know, that you are the Holy One of God.

Jesus answered them:

♦ *Did I not choose you, the twelve, and one of you is a devil?*

He spoke of Judas the son of Simon Iscariot, for he, one of the twelve, was to betray him.

(John 6, 24 – 71)

5. THE SIGNS OF JESUS BETWEEN THE THIRD PASSOVER AND HIS TRIUMPHANT ENTRY INTO JERUSALEM

5.1 *In Galilee*

A Canaanite Woman's Faith

nd Jesus went away from there and withdrew to the district of Tyre and Sidon. And behold, a Canaanite woman from that region came out and cried:

♦ *Have mercy on me, O Lord, Son of David; my daughter is severely possessed by a demon.*

But he did not answer her a word. And his disciples came and begged him, saying:

♦ *Send her away, for she is crying after us.*

He answered:

♦ *I was sent only to the lost sheep of the house of Israel.*

42

But she came and knelt before him, saying:

♦ *Lord, help me.*

And he answered:

♦ *It is not fair to take the children's bread and throw it to the dogs.*

She said:

♦ *Yes, Lord, yet even the dogs eat the crumbs that fall from their masters' table.*

Then Jesus answered her:

♦ *O woman, great is your faith! Be it done for you as you desire.*

And her daughter was healed instantly.

(Matthew 15, 21 - 28; Mark 7, 24 – 30)

Jesus Heals a Deaf and Mute Man

hen he returned from the region of Tyre, and went through Sidon to the Sea of Galilee, through the region of the Decapolis. And they brought to him a man who was deaf and had an impediment in his speech; and they besought him to lay his hand upon him. And taking him aside from the multitude privately, he put his fingers into his ears, and he spat and touched his tongue; and looking up to heaven, he sighed, and said to him:

♦ *Ephphatha*

that is:

♦ *Be opened.*

43

And his ears were opened, his tongue was released, and he spoke plainly. And he charged them to tell no one; but the more he charged them, the more zealously they proclaimed it. And they were astonished beyond measure, saying:

♦ *He has done all things well; he even makes the deaf hear and the dumb speak.*

(Mark 7, 31 – 37)

Jesus Feeds Four Thousand Men

nd Jesus went on from there and passed along the Sea of Galilee. And he went up on the mountain, and sat down there. And great crowds came to him, bringing with them the lame, the maimed, the blind, the dumb, and many others, and they put them at his feet, and he healed them, so that the throng wondered, when they saw the dumb speaking, the maimed whole, the lame walking, and the blind seeing; and they glorified the God of Israel.

Then Jesus called his disciples to him and said:

♦ *I have compassion on the crowd, because they have been with me now three days, and have nothing to eat; and I am unwilling to send them away hungry, lest they faint on the way.*

And the disciples said to him:

♦ *Where are we to get bread enough in the desert to feed so great a crowd?*

And Jesus said to them:

♦ *How many loaves have you?*

44

They said:

♦ *Seven, and a few small fish.*

And commanding the crowd to sit down on the ground, he took the seven loaves and the fish, and having given thanks he broke them and gave them to the disciples, and the disciples gave them to the crowds. And they all ate and were satisfied; and they took up seven baskets full of the broken pieces left over. Those who ate were four thousand men, besides women and children.

(Matthew 15, 29 - 38;   Mark 8, 1 – 9)

Jesus Heals a Blind Man at Bethsaida

nd they came to Bethsaida. And some people brought to him a blind man, and begged him to touch him. And he took the blind man by the hand, and led him out of the village; and when he had spit on his eyes and laid his hands upon him, he asked him:

♦ *Do you see anything?*

And he looked up and said:

♦ *I see men; but they look like trees, walking.*

Then again he laid his hands upon his eyes; and he looked intently and was restored, and saw everything clearly. And he sent him away to his home, saying:

♦ *Do not even enter the village.*

(Mark 8, 22 – 26)

The Sign of Jonah

nd the Pharisees and Sad'ducees came, and to test him they asked him to show them a sign from heaven. He answered them:

♦ *When it is evening, you say, `It will be fair weather; for the sky is red.' And in the morning, `It will be stormy today, for the sky is red and threatening.' You know how to interpret the appearance of sky, but you cannot interpret the signs of the times.*

An evil and adulterous generation seeks for a sign, but no sign shall be given to it except the sign of Jonah.

So he left them and departed. When the disciples reached the other side, they had forgotten to bring any bread. Jesus said to them:

♦ *Take heed and beware of the leaven of the Pharisees and Sadducees.*

And they discussed it among themselves, saying:

♦ *We brought no bread.*

But Jesus, aware of this, said:

♦ *O men of little faith, why do you discuss among yourselves the fact that you have no bread? Do you not yet perceive? Do you not remember the five loaves of the five thousand, and how many baskets you gathered? Or the seven loaves of the four thousand, and how many baskets you gathered? How is it that you fail to perceive that I did not speak about bread? Beware of the leaven of the Pharisees and Sadducees.*

Then they understood that he did not tell them to beware of the leaven

46

of bread, but of the teaching of the Pharisees and Sadducees.

(Matthew 16, 1 - 12;   Mark 8, 11 – 21;   Luke 12, 54 – 56)

Jesus Is the Messiah, the Son of the Living God

ow when Jesus came into the district of Caesarea Philippi, he asked his disciples:

♦ *Who do men say that the Son of man is?*

And they said:

♦ *Some say John the Baptist, others say Elijah, and others Jeremiah or one of the prophets.*

He said to them:

♦ *But who do you say that I am?*

Simon Peter replied:

♦ *You are the Christ, the Son of the living God.*

And Jesus answered him:

♦ *Blessed are you, Simon Bar-Jona! For flesh and blood has not revealed this to you, but my Father who is in heaven.*

And I tell you, you are Peter, and on this rock I will build my church, and the powers of death shall not prevail against it.

I will give you the keys of the kingdom of heaven, and whatever you bind on earth shall be bound in heaven, and whatever you loose on earth shall be loosed in heaven.

47

Then he strictly charged the disciples to tell no one that he was the Christ.

(Matthew 16, 13 - 20;   Mark 8, 27 – 30;   Luke 9, 18 – 21;
 John 6, 69)

Jesus Predicts His Death

rom that time Jesus began to show his disciples that he must go to Jerusalem and suffer many things from the elders and chief priests and scribes, and be killed, and on the third day be raised. And Peter took him and began to rebuke him, saying:

♦ *God forbid, Lord! This shall never happen to you.*

But he turned and said to Peter:

♦ *Get behind me, Satan! You are a hindrance to me; for you are not on the side of God, but of men.*

(Matthew 16, 21 - 23;   Mark 8, 31 – 33)

The Transfiguration

nd after six days Jesus took with him Peter and James and John his brother, and led them up a high mountain apart. And he was transfigured before them, and his face shone like the sun, and his garments became white as light. And behold, there appeared to them Moses and Elijah, talking with him. And Peter said to Jesus:

♦ *Lord, it is well that we are here; if you wish, I will make three booths here, one for you and one for Moses and one for Elijah.*

He was still speaking, when lo, a bright cloud overshadowed them,

48

and a voice from the cloud said:

♦ *This is my beloved Son, with whom I am well pleased; listen to him.*

When the disciples heard this, they fell on their faces, and were filled with awe. But Jesus came and touched them, saying:

♦ *Rise, and have no fear.*

And when they lifted up their eyes, they saw no one but Jesus only. And as they were coming down the mountain, Jesus commanded them:

♦ *Tell no one the vision, until the Son of man is raised from the dead.*

(Matthew 17, 1 - 9;   Mark 9, 2 – 9;   Luke 9, 28 – 36)

All Things Can Be Done for the One Who Believes

nd when they came to the disciples, they saw a great crowd about them, and scribes arguing with them. And immediately all the crowd, when they saw him, were greatly amazed, and ran up to him and greeted him. And he asked them:

♦ *What are you discussing with them?*

And one of the crowd answered him:

♦ *Teacher, I brought my son to you, for he has a dumb spirit; and wherever it seizes him, it dashes him down; and he foams and grinds his teeth and becomes rigid; and I asked your disciples to cast it out, and they were not able.*

And he answered them:

♦ *O faithless generation, how long am I to be with you? How long*

49

am I to bear with you? Bring him to me.

And they brought the boy to him; and when the spirit saw him, immediately it convulsed the boy, and he fell on the ground and rolled about, foaming at the mouth. And Jesus asked his father:

♦ *How long has he had this?*

And he said:

♦ *From childhood. And it has often cast him into the fire and into the water, to destroy him; but if you can do anything, have pity on us and help us.*

And Jesus said to him:

♦ *If you can! All things are possible to him who believes.*

Immediately the father of the child cried out and said:

♦ *I believe; help my unbelief!*

And when Jesus saw that a crowd came running together, he rebuked the unclean spirit, saying to it:

♦ *You dumb and deaf spirit, I command you, come out of him, and never enter him again.*

And after crying out and convulsing him terribly, it came out, and the boy was like a corpse; so that most of them said:

♦ *He is dead.*

But Jesus took him by the hand and lifted him up, and he arose.

(Mark 9, 14 – 27; Matthew 17, 14 - 18; Luke 9, 37 – 43)

50

Jesus Predicts His Death Again

s they were gathering in Galilee, Jesus said to them:

♦ *The Son of man is to be delivered into the hands of men, and they will kill him, and he will be raised on the third day.*

And they were greatly distressed.

(Matthew 17, 22 - 23; Mark 9, 30 – 32; Luke 9, 43 – 45)

Payment of the Temple Tax

hen they came to Capernaum, the collectors of the half-she-kel tax went up to Peter and said:

♦ *Does not your teacher pay the tax?*

He said:

♦ *Yes.*

And when he came home, Jesus spoke to him first, saying:

♦ *What do you think, Simon? From whom do kings of the earth take toll or tribute? From their sons or from others?*

And when he said:

♦ *From others,*

Jesus said to him:

♦ *Then the sons are free. However, not to give offense to them, go to the sea and cast a hook, and take the first fish that comes up, and*

51

when you open its mouth you will find a shekel; take that and give it to them for me and for yourself.

(Matthew 17, 24 – 27)

5.2 *The Journey to Jerusalem*

Jesus Has Not Come to Destroy the Lives of Human Beings but to Save Them

hen the days drew near for him to be received up, he set his face to go to Jerusalem. And he sent messengers ahead of him, who went and entered a village of the Samaritans, to make ready for him; but the people would not receive him, because his face was set toward Jerusalem. And when his disciples James and John saw it, they said:

♦ *Lord, do you want us to bid fire come down from heaven and consume them?*

But he turned and rebuked them [and said:

♦ *You do not know what spirit you are of, for the Son of Man has not come to destroy the lives of human beings but to save them.*]

And they went on to another village.

(Luke 9, 51 – 56)

Jesus Sends Out the Seventy-two

fter this the Lord appointed seventy others, and sent them on ahead of him, two by two, into every town and place where he himself was about to come. And he said to them:

♦ *The harvest is plentiful, but the laborers are few; pray therefore the Lord of the harvest to send out laborers into his harvest.*

Go your way; behold, I send you out as lambs in the midst of wolves. Carry no purse, no bag, no sandals; and salute no one on the road. Whatever house you enter, first say, `Peace be to this house!' And if a son of peace is there, your peace shall rest upon him; but if not, it shall return to you. And remain in the same house, eating and drink-ing what they provide, for the laborer deserves his wages; do not go from house to house. Whenever you enter a town and they receive you, eat what is set before you; heal the sick in it and say to them, `The kingdom of God has come near to you.' But whenever you enter a town and they do not receive you, go into its streets and say, `Even the dust of your town that clings to our feet, we wipe off against you; nevertheless know this, that the kingdom of God has come near.' I tell you, it shall be more tolerable on that day for Sodom than for that town.

Woe to you, Chorazin! woe to you, Bethsaida! for if the mighty works done in you had been done in Tyre and Sidon, they would have repented long ago, sitting in sackcloth and ashes. But it shall be more tolerable in the judgment for Tyre and Sidon than for you. And you, Capernaum, will you be exalted to heaven? You shall be brought down to Hades.

He who hears you hears me, and he who rejects you rejects me, and he who rejects me rejects him who sent me.

The seventy returned with joy, saying:

♦ *Lord, even the demons are subject to us in your name!*

And he said to them:

♦ I *saw Satan fall like lightning from heaven. Behold, I have given*

53

you authority to tread upon serpents and scorpions, and over all the power of the enemy; and nothing shall hurt you. Nevertheless do not rejoice in this, that the spirits are subject to you; but rejoice that your names are written in heaven.

In that same hour he rejoiced in the Holy Spirit and said:

♦ *I thank thee, Father, Lord of heaven and earth, that thou hast hidden these things from the wise and understanding and revealed them to babes; yea, Father, for such was thy gracious will. All things have been delivered to me by my Father; and no one knows who the Son is except the Father, or who the Father is except the Son and any one to whom the Son chooses to reveal him.*

Then turning to the disciples he said privately:

♦ *Blessed are the eyes which see what you see! For I tell you that many prophets and kings desired to see what you see, and did not see it, and to hear what you hear, and did not hear it.*

(Luke 10, 1 – 24; Matthew 9, 37. 38; 10, 9 - 16; Mark 6, 8 – 11)

Jesus Goes to the Feast of Booths (Tabernacles)

fter this Jesus went about in Galilee; he would not go about in Judea, because the Jews sought to kill him. Now the Jews' feast of Tabernacles was at hand. So his brothers said to him:

♦ *Leave here and go to Judea, that your disciples may see the works you are doing. For no man works in secret if he seeks to be known openly. If you do these things, show yourself to the world.*

For even his brothers did not believe in him. Jesus said to them:

54

♦ *My time has not yet come, but your time is always here. The world cannot hate you, but it hates me because I testify of it that its works are evil. Go to the feast yourselves; I am not going up to this feast, for my time has not yet fully come.*

So saying, he remained in Galilee. But after his brothers had gone up to the feast, then he also went up, not publicly but in private. The Jews were looking for him at the feast, and saying:

♦ *Where is he?*

And there was much muttering about him among the people. While some said:

♦ *He is a good man,*

others said:

♦ *No, he is leading the people astray.*

Yet for fear of the Jews no one spoke openly of him.

(John 7, 1 – 13)

5.3 In Jerusalem

Jesus at the Festival of Booths (Tabernacles)

bout the middle of the feast Jesus went up into the temple and taught. The Jews marveled at it, saying:

♦ *How is it that this man has learning, when he has never studied?*

So Jesus answered them:

♦ *My teaching is not mine, but his who sent me; if any man's will is to do his will, he shall know whether the teaching is from God or whether I am speaking on my own authority. He who speaks on his own authority seeks his own glory; but he who seeks the glory of him who sent him is true, and in him there is no falsehood.*

Did not Moses give you the law? Yet none of you keeps the law. Why do you seek to kill me?

The people answered:

♦ *You have a demon! Who is seeking to kill you?*

Jesus answered them:

♦ *I did one deed, and you all marvel at it. Moses gave you circumcision (not that it is from Moses, but from the fathers), and you circumcise a man upon the sabbath. If on the sabbath a man receives circumcision, so that the law of Moses may not be broken, are you angry with me because on the sabbath I made a man's whole body well? Do not judge by appearances, but judge with right judgment.*

Some of the people of Jerusalem therefore said:

♦ *Is not this the man whom they seek to kill? And here he is, speaking openly, and they say nothing to him! Can it be that the authorities really know that this is the Christ? Yet we know where this man comes from; and when the Christ appears, no one will know where he comes from.*

So Jesus proclaimed, as he taught in the temple:

♦ *You know me, and you know where I come from? But I have not come of my own accord; he who sent me is true, and him you do not know. I know him, for I come from him, and he sent me.*

So they sought to arrest him; but no one laid hands on him, because his hour had not yet come. Yet many of the people believed in him; they said:

♦ *When the Christ appears, will he do more signs than this man has done?*

The Pharisees heard the crowd thus muttering about him, and the chief priests and Pharisees sent officers to arrest him. Jesus then said:

♦ *I shall be with you a little longer, and then I go to him who sent me; you will seek me and you will not find me; where I am you cannot come.*

The Jews said to one another:

♦ *Where does this man intend to go that we shall not find him? Does he intend to go to the Dispersion among the Greeks and teach the Greeks? What does he mean by saying, `You will seek me and you will not find me,' and, `Where I am you cannot come'?*

On the last day of the feast, the great day, Jesus stood up and proclaimed:

♦ *If any one thirst, let him come to me and drink. He who believes in me, as the scripture has said, `Out of his heart shall flow rivers of living water.'*

Now this he said about the Spirit, which those who believed in him were to receive; for as yet the Spirit had not been given, because Jesus was not yet glorified. When they heard these words, some of the people said:

♦ *This is really the prophet.*

Others said:

57

♦ *This is the Christ.*

But some said:

♦ *Is the Christ to come from Galilee? Has not the scripture said that the Christ is descended from David, and comes from Bethlehem, the village where David was?*

So there was a division among the people over him. Some of them wanted to arrest him, but no one laid hands on him.

(John 7, 14 – 44)

Whoever Keeps Jesus' Word Will Never See Death

gain he (Jesus) said to them (the Jews):

♦ *I go away, and you will seek me and die in your sin; where I am going, you cannot come.*

Then said the Jews:

♦ *Will he kill himself, since he says, `Where I am going, you cannot come'?*

He said to them:

♦ *You are from below, I am from above; you are of this world, I am not of this world. I told you that you would die in your sins, for you will die in your sins unless you believe that I am he.*

They said to him:

♦ *Who are you?*

Jesus said to them:

58

♦ *Even what I have told you from the beginning. I have much to say about you and much to judge; but he who sent me is true, and I declare to the world what I have heard from him.*

They did not understand that he spoke to them of the Father. So Jesus said

♦ *When you have lifted up the Son of man, then you will know that I am he, and that I do nothing on my own authority but speak thus as the Father taught me. And he who sent me is with me; he has not left me alone, for I always do what is pleasing to him.*

As he spoke thus, many believed in him. Jesus then said to the Jews who had believed in him:

♦ *If you continue in my word, you are truly my disciples, and you will wiknow the truth, and the truth will make you free.*

They answered him:

♦ *We are descendants of Abraham, and have never been in bondage to any one. How is it that you say, `You will be made free'?*

Jesus answered them:

♦ *Truly, truly, I say to you, every one who commits sin is a slave to sin. The slave does not continue in the house for ever; the son continues for ever. So if the Son makes you free, you will be free indeed. I know that you are descendants of Abraham; yet you seek to kill me, because my word finds no place in you. I speak of what I have seen with my Father, and you do what you have heard from your father.*

They answered him:

♦ *Abraham is our father.*

Jesus said to them:

♦ *If you were Abraham's children, you would do what Abraham did, but now you seek to kill me, a man who has told you the truth which I heard from God; this is not what Abraham did. You do what your father did.*

They said to him:

♦ *We were not born of fornication; we have one Father, even God.*

Jesus said to them:

♦ *If God were your Father, you would love me, for I proceeded and came forth from God; I came not of my own accord, but he sent me. Why do you not understand what I say? It is because you cannot bear to hear my word. You are of your father the devil, and your will is to do your father's desires. He was a murderer from the beginning, and has nothing to do with the truth, because there is no truth in him. When he lies, he speaks according to his own nature, for he is a liar and the father of lies. But, because I tell the truth, you do not believe me. Which of you convicts me of sin? If I tell the truth, why do you not believe me? He who is of God hears the words of God; the reason why you do not hear them is that you are no of God.*

The Jews answered him:

♦ *Are we not right in saying that you are a Samaritan and have a demon?*

Jesus answered:

♦ *I have not a demon; but I honor my Father, and you dishonor me. Yet I do not seek my own glory; there is One who seeks it and he will be the judge. Truly, truly, I say to you, if any one keeps my word, he will never see death.*

The Jews said to him:

♦ *Now we know that you have a demon. Abraham died, as did the prophets; and you say, `If any one keeps my word, he will never taste death.' Are you greater than our father Abraham, who died? And the prophets died! Who do you claim to be?*

Jesus answered:

♦ *If I glorify myself, my glory is nothing; it is my Father who glorifies me, of whom you say that he is your God. But you have not known him; I know him. If I said, I do not know him, I should be a liar like you; but I do know him and I keep his word. Your father Abraham rejoiced that he was to see my day; he saw it and was glad.*

The Jews then said to him:

♦ *You are not yet fifty years old, and have you seen Abraham?*

Jesus said to them:

♦ *Truly, truly, I say to you, before Abraham was, I am.*

So they took up stones to throw at him; but Jesus hid himself, and went out of the temple.

(John 8, 21 – 59)

Jesus Heals a Man Born Blind

s he passed by, he (Jesus) saw a man blind from his birth. And his disciples asked him:

♦ *Rabbi, who sinned, this man or his parents, that he was born blind?*

Jesus answered:

♦ *It was not that this man sinned, or his parents, but that the works of God might be made manifest in him. We must work the works of him who sent me, while it is day; night comes, when no one can work. As long as I am in the world, I am the light of the world.*

As he said this, he spat on the ground and made clay of the spittle and anointed the man's eyes with the clay, saying to him:

♦ *Go, wash in the pool of Siloam* (which means Sent).

So he went and washed and came back seeing. The neighbors and those who had seen him before as a beggar, said:

♦ *Is not this the man who used to sit and beg?*

Some said:

♦ *It is he.*

Others said:

♦ *No, but he is like him.*

He said:

♦ *I am the man.*

They said to him:

♦ *Then how were your eyes opened?*

He answered:

♦ *The man called Jesus made clay and anointed my eyes and said to me, `Go to Siloam and wash'; so I went and washed and received my sight.*

They said to him:

♦ *Where is he?*

He said:

♦ *I do not know.*

They brought to the Pharisees the man who had formerly been blind. Now it was a sabbath day when Jesus made the clay and opened his eyes. The Pharisees again asked him how he had received his sight. And he said to them:

♦ *He put clay on my eyes, and I washed, and I see.*

Some of the Pharisees said:

♦ *This man is not from God, for he does not keep the sabbath.*

But others said:

♦ *How can a man who is a sinner do such signs?*

There was a division among them. So they again said to the blind man:

♦ *What do you say about him, since he has opened your eyes?*

He said:

♦ *He is a prophet.*

The Jews did not believe that he had been blind and had received his sight, until they called the parents of the man who had received his sight, and asked them:

♦ *Is this your son, who you say was born blind? How then does he now see?*

His parents answered:

♦ *We know that this is our son, and that he was born blind; but how he now sees we do not know, nor do we know who opened his eyes. Ask him; he is of age, he will speak for himself.*

His parents said this because they feared the Jews, for the Jews had already agreed that if any one should confess him to be Christ, he was to be put out of the synagogue. Therefore his parents said:

♦ *He is of age; ask him.*

So for the second time they called the man who had been blind, and they said to him:

♦ *Give God the praise; we know that this man is a sinner.*

He answered:

♦ *Whether he is a sinner, I do not know; one thing I know, that though I was blind, now I see.*

They said to him:

♦ *What did he do to you? How did he open your eyes?*

He answered them:

♦ *I have told you already, and you would not listen. Why do you want to hear it again? Do you too want to become his disciples?*

And they reviled him, saying:

♦ *You are his disciple, but we are disciples of Moses. We know that God has spoken to Moses, but as for this man, we do not know where he comes from.*

The man answered:

♦ *Why, this is a marvel! You do not know where he comes from, and yet he opened my eyes. We know that God does not listen to sinners, but if any one is a worshiper of God and does his will, God listens to him. Never since the world began has it been heard that any one opened the eyes of a man born blind. If this man were not from God, he could do nothing.*

They answered him:

♦ *You were born in utter sin, and would you teach us?*

And they cast him out. Jesus heard that they had cast him out, and having found him he said:

♦ *Do you believe in the Son of man?*

He answered:

♦ *And who is he, sir, that I may believe in him?*

Jesus said to him:

♦ *You have seen him, and it is he who speaks to you.*

He said:

♦ *Lord, I believe.*

And he worshipped him.

(John 9, 1 – 38)

5.4 *In Galilee and on the Journey to Jerusalem*

Jesus Heals a Crippled Woman on the Sabbath

Now he was teaching in one of the synagogues on the sabbath. And there was a woman who had had a spirit of infirmity for eighteen years; she was bent over and could not fully straighten herself. And when Jesus saw her, he called her and said to her:

♦ *Woman, you are freed from your infirmity.*

And he laid his hands upon her, and immediately she was made straight, and she praised God. But the ruler of the synagogue, indignant because Jesus had healed on the sabbath, said to the people:

♦ *There are six days on which work ought to be done; come on those days and be healed, and not on the sabbath day.*

Then the Lord answered him:

♦ *You hypocrites! Does not each of you on the sabbath untie his ox or his ass from the manger, and lead it away to water it? And ought not this woman, a daughter of Abraham whom Satan bound for eighteen years, be loosed from this bond on the sabbath day?*

As he said this, all his adversaries were put to shame; and all the people rejoiced at all the glorious things that were done by him.

(Luke 13, 10 – 17)

Jesus Heals a Man With Dropsy
on the Sabbath

ne sabbath when he went to dine at the house of a ruler who belonged to the Pharisees, they were watching him. And behold, there was a man before him who had dropsy.

And Jesus spoke to the lawyers and Pharisees, saying:

♦ *Is it lawful to heal on the sabbath, or not?*

But they were silent. Then he took him and healed him, and let him go. And he said to them:

♦ *Which of you, having a son or an ox that has fallen into a well, will not immediately pull him out on a sabbath day?*

And they could not reply to this.

(Luke 14, 1 – 6)

Jesus Heals Ten Lepers

n the way to Jerusalem he was passing along between Samaria and Galilee. And as he entered a village, he was met by ten lepers, who stood at a distance and lifted up their voices and said:

♦ *Jesus, Master, have mercy on us!*

When he saw them, he said to them:

♦ *Go and show yourselves to the priests.*

And as they went they were cleansed. Then one of them, when he saw that he was healed, turned back, praising God with a loud voice; and he fell on his face at Jesus' feet, giving him thanks. Now he was a Samaritan:

♦ *Were not ten cleansed? Where are the nine? Was no one found to return and give praise to God except this foreigner?*

Then said Jesus:

♦ *Rise and go your way; your faith has made you well.*

(Luke 17, 11 – 19)

5.5 *In Jerusalem*

The Father and Jesus Are One

t was the feast of the Dedication at Jerusalem; it was winter, and Jesus was walking in the temple, in the portico of Solomon. So the Jews gathered round him and said to him:

♦ *How long will you keep us in suspense? If you are the Christ, tell us plainly.*

Jesus answered them:

♦ *I told you, and you do not believe. The works that I do in my Father's name, they bear witness to me; but you do not believe, because you do not belong to my sheep. My sheep hear my voice, and I know them, and they follow me; and I give them eternal life, and they shall never perish, and no one shall snatch them out of my hand. My Father, who has given them to me, is greater than all,*

68

and no one is able to snatch them out of the Father's hand. I and the Father are one.

The Jews took up stones again to stone him. Jesus answered them:

♦ *I have shown you many good works from the Father; for which of these do you stone me?*

The Jews answered him:

♦ *It is not for a good work that we stone you but for blasphemy; because you, being a man, make yourself God.*

Jesus answered them:

♦ *Is it not written in your law, `I said, you are gods'? If he called them gods to whom the word of God came (and scripture cannot be broken), do you say of him whom the Father consecrated and sent into the world, `You are blaspheming,' because I said, `I am the Son of God'? If I am not doing the works of my Father, then do not believe me; but if I do them, even though you do not believe me, believe the works, that you may know and understand that the Father is in me and I am in the Father.*

Again they tried to arrest him, but he escaped from their hands. He went away again across the Jordan to the place where John at first baptized, and there he remained. And many came to him; and they said:

♦ *John did no sign, but everything that John said about this man was true.*

And many believed in him there.

(John 10, 22 – 42)

69

5.6 In Judea

Jesus Raises Lazarus from the Dead

ow a certain man was ill, Lazarus of Bethany, the village of Mary and her sister Martha. It was Mary who anointed the Lord with ointment and wiped his feet with her hair, whose brother Lazarus was ill. So the sisters sent to him, saying:

♦ *Lord, he whom you love is ill.*

But when Jesus heard it, he said:

♦ *This illness is not unto death; it is for the glory of God, so that the Son of God may be glorified by means of it.*

Now Jesus loved Martha and her sister and Lazarus. So when he heard that he was ill, he stayed two days longer in the place where he was. Then after this he said to the disciples:

♦ *Let us go into Judea again.*

The disciples said to him:

♦ *Rabbi, the Jews were but now seeking to stone you, and are you going there again?*

Jesus answered:

♦ *Are there not twelve hours in the day? If any one walks in the day, he does not stumble, because he sees the light of this world. But if any one walks in the night, he stumbles, because the light is not in him.*

Thus he spoke, and then he said to them:

♦ *Our friend Lazarus has fallen asleep, but I go to awake him out of sleep.*

The disciples said to him:

♦ *Lord, if he has fallen asleep, he will recover.*

Now Jesus had spoken of his death, but they thought that he meant taking rest in sleep. Then Jesus told them plainly:

♦ *Lazarus is dead; and for your sake I am glad that I was not there, so that you may believe. But let us go to him.*

Thomas, called the Twin, said to his fellow disciples:

♦ *Let us also go, that we may die with him.*

Now when Jesus came, he found that Lazarus had already been in the tomb four days. Bethany was near Jerusalem, about two miles off, and many of the Jews had come to Martha and Mary to console them concerning their brother. When Martha heard that Jesus was coming, she went and met him, while Mary sat in the house. Martha said to Jesus:

♦ *Lord, if you had been here, my brother would not have died. And even now I know that whatever you ask from God, God will give you.*

Jesus said to her:

♦ *Your brother will rise again.*

Martha said to him:

♦ *I know that he will rise again in the resurrection at the last day.*

Jesus said to her:

♦ *I am the resurrection and the life; he who believes in me, though he die, yet shall he live, and whoever lives and believes in me shall never die. Do you believe this?*

She said to him:

♦ *Yes, Lord; I believe that you are the Christ, the Son of God, he who is coming into the world.*

When she had said this, she went and called her sister Mary, saying quietly:

♦ *The Teacher is here and is calling for you.*

And when she heard it, she rose quickly and went to him. Now Jesus had not yet come to the village, but was still in the place where Martha had met him. When the Jews who were with her in the house, consoling her, saw Mary rise quickly and go out, they followed her, supposing that she was going to the tomb to weep there. Then Mary, when she came where Jesus was and saw him, fell at his feet, saying to him:

♦ *Lord, if you had been here, my brother would not have died.*

When Jesus saw her weeping, and the Jews who came with her also weeping, he was deeply moved in spirit and troubled; and he said:

♦ *Where have you laid him?*

They said to him:

♦ *Lord, come and see.*

Jesus wept. So the Jews said:

♦ *See how he loved him!*

But some of them said:

♦ *Could not he who opened the eyes of the blind man have kept this man from dying?*

Then Jesus, deeply moved again, came to the tomb; it was a cave, and a stone lay upon it. Jesus said:

♦ *Take away the stone.*

Martha, the sister of the dead man, said to him:

♦ *Lord, by this time there will be an odor, for he has been dead four days.*

Jesus said to her:

♦ *Did I not tell you that if you would believe you would see the glory of God?*

So they took away the stone. And Jesus lifted up his eyes and said:

♦ *Father, I thank thee that thou hast heard me. I knew that thou hearest me always, but I have said this on account of the people standing by, that they may believe that thou didst send me.*

When he had said this, he cried with a loud voice:

♦ *Lazarus, come out.*

The dead man came out, his hands and feet bound with bandages, and his face wrapped with a cloth. Jesus said to them:

♦ *Unbind him, and let him go.*

Many of the Jews therefore, who had come with Mary and had seen

73

what he did, believed in him; but some of them went to the Pharisees and told them what Jesus had done.

(John 11, 1 - 46)

Jesus Anointed for His Burial

ix days before the Passover, Jesus came to Bethany, where Lazarus was, whom Jesus had raised from the dead. There they made him a supper; Martha served, and Lazarus was one of those at table with him. Mary took a pound of costly ointment of pure nard and anointed the feet of Jesus and wiped his feet with her hair; and the house was filled with the fragrance of the ointment.

But Judas Iscariot, one of his disciples (he who was to betray him), said:

♦ *Why was this ointment not sold for three hundred denarii and given to the poor?*

This he said, not that he cared for the poor but because he was a thief, and as he had the money box he used to take what was put into it. Jesus said:

♦ *Let her alone, let her keep it for the day of my burial. The poor you always have with you, but you do not always have me.*

When the great crowd of the Jews learned that he was there, they came, not only on account of Jesus but also to see Lazarus, whom he had raised from the dead. So the chief priests planned to put Lazarus also to death, because on account of him many of the Jews were going away and believing in Jesus.

(John 12, 1 – 11; Matthew 26, 6 – 13; Mark 14, 3 – 9)

Jesus Heals Blind Bartimaeus

nd they came to Jericho; and as he was leaving Jericho with his disciples and a great multitude, Bartimaeus, a blind beggar, the son of Timaeus, was sitting by the roadside. And when he heard that it was Jesus of Nazareth, he began to cry out and say:

♦ *Jesus, Son of David, have mercy on me!*

And many rebuked him, telling him to be silent; but he cried out all the more:

♦ *Son of David, have mercy on me!*

And Jesus stopped and said:

♦ *Call him.*

And they called the blind man, saying to him:

♦ *Take heart; rise, he is calling you.*

And throwing off his mantle he sprang up and came to Jesus. And Jesus said to him:

♦ *What do you want me to do for you?*

And the blind man said to him:

♦ *Master, let me receive my sight.*

And Jesus said to him:

♦ *Go your way; your faith has made you well.*

75

And immediately he received his sight and followed him on the way.

(Mark 10, 46 – 52;   Luke 18, 35 – 43;   Matthew 20, 29 - 34)

6. THE LAST SIGNS OF JESUS

Preparing for the Triumphant
Entry into Jerusalem

nd when they drew near to Jerusalem and came to Bethphage, to the Mount of Olives, then Jesus sent two disciples, saying to them:

♦ *Go into the village opposite you, and immediately you will find an ass tied, and a colt with her; untie them and bring them to me. If any one says anything to you, you shall say, 'The Lord has need of them,' and he will send them immediately.*

(Matthew 21, 1 – 3;   Mark 11, 1 – 3;   Luke 19, 29 - 31)

The Triumphant Entry into Jerusalem

hen the great crowd of the Jews learned that he was there, they came, not only on account of Jesus but also to see Lazarus, whom he had raised from the dead. So the chief priests planned to put Lazarus also to death, because on account of him many of the Jews were going away and believing in Jesus. The next day a great crowd who had come to the feast heard that Jesus was coming to Jerusalem. So they took branches of palm trees and went out to meet him, crying:

♦ *Hosanna! Blessed is he who comes in the name of the Lord, even the King of Israel!*

And Jesus found a young ass and sat upon it; as it is written:

♦ *Fear not, daughter of Zion; behold, your king is coming, sitting on an ass's colt!*

His disciples did not understand this at first; but when Jesus was glorified, then they remembered that this had been written of him and had been done to him. The crowd that had been with him when he called Lazarus out of the tomb and raised him from the dead bore witness. The reason why the crowd went to meet him was that they heard he had done this sign. The Pharisees then said to one another:

♦ *You see that you can do nothing; look, the world has gone after him.*

Now among those who went up to worship at the feast were some Greeks. So these came to Philip, who was from Bethsaida in Galilee, and said to him:

♦ *Sir, we wish to see Jesus.*

Philip went and told Andrew; Andrew went with Philip and they told Jesus. And Jesus answered them:

♦ *The hour has come for the Son of man to be glorified. Truly, truly, I say to you, unless a grain of wheat falls into the earth and dies, it remains alone; but if it dies, it bears much fruit.*

He who loves his life loses it, and he who hates his life in this world will keep it for eternal life.

If any one serves me, he must follow me; and where I am, there shall my servant be also; if any one serves me, the Father will honor him.

Now is my soul troubled. And what shall I say? `Father, save me from this hour'? No, for this purpose I have come to this hour. Father, glorify thy name.

Then a voice came from heaven:

♦ *I have glorified it, and I will glorify it again.*

The crowd standing by heard it and said that it had thundered. Others said:

♦ *An angel has spoken to him.*

Jesus answered:

♦ *This voice has come for your sake, not for mine. Now is the judgment of this world, now shall the ruler of this world be cast out; and I, when I am lifted up from the earth, will draw all men to myself.*

He said this to show by what death he was to die. The crowd answered him:

♦ *We have heard from the law that the Christ remains for ever. How can you say that the Son of man must be lifted up? Who is this Son of man?*

Jesus said to them:

♦ *The light is with you for a little longer. Walk while you have the light, lest the darkness overtake you; he who walks in the darkness does not know where he goes. While you have the light, believe in the light, that you may become sons of light.*

When Jesus had said this, he departed and hid himself from them. Though he had done so many signs before them, yet they did not believe in him; it was that the word spoken by the prophet Isaiah might be fulfilled:

♦ *Lord, who has believed our report, and to whom has the arm of the Lord been revealed?*

Therefore they could not believe. For Isaiah again said:

78

♦ *He has blinded their eyes and hardened their heart, lest they should see with their eyes and perceive with their heart, and turn for me to heal them.*

Isaiah said this because he saw his glory and spoke of him. Nevertheless many even of the authorities believed in him, but for fear of the Pharisees they did not confess it, lest they should be put out of the synagogue: for they loved the praise of men more than the praise of God. And Jesus cried out and said:

♦ *He who believes in me, believes not in me but in him who sent me. And he who sees me sees him who sent me. I have come as light into the world, that whoever believes in me may not remain in darkness. If any one hears my sayings and does not keep them, I do not judge him; for I did not come to judge the world but to save the world. He who rejects me and does not receive my sayings has a judge; the word that I have spoken will be his judge on the last day. For I have not spoken on my own authority; the Father who sent me has himself given me commandment what to say and what to speak. And I know that his commandment is eternal life. What I say, therefore, I say as the Father has bidden me.*

(John 12, 9 – 50; Matthew 21, 8 – 9; Mark 11, 8 – 10; Luke 19, 36 – 38; Matthew 10, 39; 16, 25; Mark 8, 35; Luke 9, 24; 17; 33; Matthew 13, 14. 15; 26, 38. 39; Mark 9, 37; Luke 10, 16)

Jesus Curses the Fig Tree - Whatever You Ask for in Prayer with Faith, You Will Receive

n the morning, as he (Jesus) was returning to the city, he was hungry. And seeing a fig tree by the wayside he went to it, and found nothing on it but leaves only. And he said to it:

79

♦ *May no fruit ever come from you again!*

And the fig tree withered at once. When the disciples saw it they marveled, saying:

♦ *How did the fig tree wither at once?*

And Jesus answered them:

♦ *Truly, I say to you, if you have faith and never doubt, you will not only do what has been done to the fig tree, but even if you say to this mountain, `Be taken up and cast into the sea,' it will be done. And whatever you ask in prayer, you will receive, if you have faith.*

(Matthew 21, 18 – 22)

♦ *Have faith in God. Truly, I say to you, whoever says to this mountain, `Be taken up and cast into the sea,' and does not doubt in his heart, but believes that what he says will come to pass, it will be done for him. Therefore I tell you, whatever you ask in prayer, believe that you have received it, and it will be yours.*

(Mark 11, 22 – 24)

The Signs of Jesus' Coming and of
the End of the Age

s he (Jesus) sat on the Mount of Olives, the disciples came to him privately, saying:

♦ *Tell us, when will this be, and what will be the sign of your coming and of the close of the age?*

And Jesus answered them:

♦ *Take heed that no one leads you astray. For many will come in my* *name, saying, `I am the Christ,' and they will lead many astray.*

And you will hear of wars and rumors of wars; see that you are not alarmed; for this must take place, but the end is not yet. For nation will rise against nation, and kingdom against kingdom, and there will be famines and earthquakes in various places: all this is but the beginning of the birth-pangs.

Then they will deliver you up to tribulation, and put you to death; and you will be hated by all nations for my name's sake. And then many will fall away, and betray one another, and hate one another. And many false prophets will arise and lead many astray. And because wickedness is multiplied, most men's love will grow cold.

But he who endures to the end will be saved.

And this gospel of the kingdom will be preached throughout the whole world, as a testimony to all nations; and then the end will come.

So when you see the desolating sacrilege spoken of by the prophet Daniel, standing in the holy place (let the reader understand), then let those who are in Judea flee to the mountains; let him who is on the housetop not go down to take what is in his house; and let him who is in the field not turn back to take his mantle. And alas for those who are with child and for those who give suck in those days! Pray that your flight may not be in winter or on a sabbath. For then there will be great tribulation, such as has not been from the beginning of the world until now, no, and never will be.

And if those days had not been shortened, no human being would be saved; but for the sake of the elect those days will be shortened.

Then if any one says to you, `Lo, here is the Christ!' or `There he is!' do not believe it. For false Christs and false prophets will arise

81

and show great signs and wonders, so as to lead astray, if possible, even the elect.

Lo, I have told you beforehand.

(Matthew 24, 3 – 25;   Mark 13, 3 – 23;   Luke 21, 7 - 19)

The Coming of the Son of Man

Jesus (to his disciples):

o, if they say to you, `Lo, he is in the wilderness,' do not go out; if they say, `Lo, he is in the inner rooms,' do not believe it. For as the lightning comes from the east and shines as far as the west, so will be the coming of the Son of man.

Wherever the body is, there the eagles will be gathered together.

Immediately after the tribulation of those days the sun will be darkened, and the moon will not give its light, and the stars will fall from heaven, and the powers of the heavens will be shaken; then will appear the sign of the Son of man in heaven, and then all the tribes of the earth will mourn, and they will see the Son of man coming on the clouds of heaven with power and great glory; and he will send out his angels with a loud trumpet call, and they will gather his elect from the four winds, from one end of heaven to the other.

From the fig tree learn its lesson: as soon as its branch becomes tender and puts forth its leaves, you know that summer is near. So also, when you see all these things, you know that he is near, at the very gates. Truly, I say to you, this generation will not pass away till all these things take place. Heaven and earth will pass away, but my words will not pass away.

(Matthew 24, 26 – 35;   Mark 13, 24 – 44)

No One Knows the Day and Hour

Jesus (to his disciples):

ut of that day and hour no one knows, not even the angels of heaven, nor the Son, but the Father only. As were the days of Noah, so will be the coming of the Son of man. For as in those days before the flood they were eating and drinking, marrying and giving in marriage, until the day when Noah entered the ark, and they did not know until the flood came and swept them all away, so will be the coming of the Son of man. Then two men will be in the field; one is taken and one is left. Two women will be grinding at the mill; one is taken and one is left. Watch therefore, for you do not know on what day your Lord is coming.

(Matthew 24, 36 – 42;   Mark 13, 32. 33; Luke 17, 26. 27.
34 - 36)

The Final Judgment

Jesus (to his disciples):

hen the Son of man comes in his glory, and all the angels with him, then he will sit on his glorious throne. Before him will be gathered all the nations, and he will separate them one from another as a shepherd separates the sheep from the goats, and he will place the sheep at his right hand, but the goats at the left.

Then the King will say to those at his right hand, `Come, O blessed of my Father, inherit the kingdom prepared for you from the foundation of the world; for I was hungry and you gave me food, I was thirsty and you gave me drink, I was a stranger and you welcomed me, I was naked and you clothed me, I was sick and you visited me, I was in prison and you came to me.'

Then the righteous will answer him, `Lord, when did we see thee hungry and feed thee, or thirsty and give thee drink? And when did we see thee a stranger and welcome thee, or naked and clothe thee? And when did we see thee sick or in prison and visit thee?'

And the King will answer them, `Truly, I say to you, as you did it to one of the least of these my brethren, you did it to me.' Then he will say to those at his left hand, `Depart from me, you cursed, into the eternal fire prepared for the devil and his angels; for I was hungry and you gave me no food, I was thirsty and you gave me no drink, I was a stranger and you did not welcome me, naked and you did not clothe me, sick and in prison and you did not visit me.'

Then they also will answer, `Lord, when did we see thee hungry or thirsty or a stranger or naked or sick or in prison, and did not minister to thee?'

Then he will answer them, `Truly, I say to you, as you did it not to one of the least of these, you did it not to me.' And they will go away into eternal punishment, but the righteous into eternal life.

(Matthew 25, 31 – 46)

The Last Supper

nd when the hour came, he sat at table, and the apostles with him. And he said to them:

♦ *I I have earnestly desired to eat this passover with you before I suffer; for I tell you I shall not eat it until it is fulfilled in the kingdom of God.*

And he took a cup, and when he had given thanks he said:

♦ *Take this, and divide it among yourselves; for I tell you that from*

*now on I shall not drink of the fruit of the vine until the kingdom
of God comes.*

And he took bread, and when he had given thanks he broke it and
gave it to them, saying:

♦ *This is my body which is given for you. Do this in remembrance
of me.*

And likewise the cup after supper, saying:

♦ *This cup which is poured out for you is the new covenant in my
blood. But behold the hand of him who betrays me is with me on
the table. For the Son of man goes as it has been determined; but
woe to that man by whom he is betrayed!*

(Luke 22, 14 – 22;   Matthew 26, 20 – 29;   Mark 14, 17 – 25)

Jesus Predicts His Betrayal

Jesus (to his disciples):

ruly, truly, I say to you, one of you will betray me.

The disciples looked at one another, uncertain of whom he
spoke. One of his disciples, whom Jesus loved, was lying
close to the breast of Jesus; so Simon Peter beckoned to him and said:

♦ *Tell us who it is of whom he speaks.*

So lying thus, close to the breast of Jesus, he said to him:

♦ *Lord, who is it?*

Jesus answered:

♦ *It is he to whom I shall give this morsel when I have dipped it.*

85

So when he had dipped the morsel, he gave it to Judas, the son of Simon Iscariot. Then after the morsel, Satan entered into him. Jesus said to him:

♦ *What you are going to do, do quickly.*

Now no one at the table knew why he said this to him. Some thought that, because Judas had the money box, Jesus was telling him:

♦ *Buy what we need for the feast;*

or, that he should give something to the poor. So, after receiving the morsel, he immediately went out; and it was night.

(John 13, 21 – 30)

Jesus' New Commandment and
Prediction of Peter's Denial (John)

hen he (Judas son of Simon Iscariot) had gone out, Jesus said:

♦ *Now is the Son of man glorified, and in him God is glorified; if God is glorified in him, God will also glorify him in himself, and glorify him at once. Little children, yet a little while I am with you. You will seek me; and as I said to the Jews so now I say to you, `Where I am going you cannot come.' A new commandment I give to you, that you love one another; even as I have loved you, that you also love one another. By this all men will know that you are my disciples, if you have love for one another.*

Simon Peter said to him:

♦ *Lord, where are you going?*

Jesus answered:

♦ *Where I am going you cannot follow me now; but you shall follow afterward.*

Peter said to him:

♦ *Lord, why cannot I follow you now? I will lay down my life for you.*

Jesus answered:

♦ *Will you lay down your life for me? Truly, truly, I say to you, the cock will not crow, till you have denied me three times.*

(John 13, 31 – 38; Matthew 26, 33. 34;   Mark 14, 29. 30;
   Luke 22, 33. 34)

Jesus Predicts the Denial of Peter and
the Disciples (Matthew)

nd when they had sung a hymn, they went out to the Mount of Olives. Then Jesus said to them:

♦ *You will all fall away because of me this night; for it is written, `I will strike the shepherd, and the sheep of the flock will be scattered.' But after I am raised up, I will go before you to Galilee.*

Peter declared to him:

♦ *Though they all fall away because of you, I will never fall away.*

Jesus said to him:

♦ *Truly, I say to you, this very night, before the cock crows, you will deny me three times.*

Peter said to him:

♦ *Even if I must die with you, I will not deny you.*

And so said all the disciples.

(Matthew 26, 30 - 35;   Mark 14, 26 - 31;   Luke 22, 33. 34)

Jesus Predicts Peter's Denial (Luke)

Jesus (to Peter):

imon, Simon, behold, Satan demanded to have you, that he might sift you like wheat, but I have prayed for you that your faith may not fail; and when you have turned again, strengthen your brethren.

And he said to him:

♦ *Lord, I am ready to go with you to prison and to death!*

He said:

♦ *I tell you, Peter, the cock will not crow this day, until you three times deny that you know me.*

(Luke 22, 31 – 34;   Matthew 26, 33 - 35;   Mark 14, 29 – 31)

The Last Supper Discourses

Jesus (to his disciples):

et not your hearts be troubled; believe in God, believe also in me. In my Father's house are many rooms; if it were not so, would I have told you that I go to prepare a place for you? And when I go and prepare a place for you, I will come again and will take you to myself, that where I am you may be also.

And you know the way where I am going.

Thomas said to him:

♦ *Lord, we do not know where you are going; how can we know the way?*

Jesus said to him:

♦ *I am the way, and the truth, and the life; no one comes to the Father, but by me. If you had known me, you would have known my Father also; henceforth you know him and have seen him.*

Philip said to him:

♦ *Lord, show us the Father, and we shall be satisfied.*

Jesus said to him:

♦ *Have I been with you so long, and yet you do not know me, Philip? He who has seen me has seen the Father; how can you say, `Show us the Father'? Do you not believe that I am in the Father and the Father in me? The words that I say to you I do not speak on my own authority; but the Father who dwells in me does his works. Believe me that I am in the Father and the Father in me; or else believe me for the sake of the works themselves.*

Truly, truly, I say to you, he who believes in me will also do the works that I do; and greater works than these will he do, because I go to the Father. Whatever you ask in my name, I will do it, that the Father may be glorified in the Son; if you ask anything in my name, I will do it.

If you love me, you will keep my commandments. And I will pray the Father, and he will give you another Counselor, to be with you for ever, even the Spirit of truth, whom the world cannot receive, because it neither sees him nor knows him; you know him, for he dwells with you, and will be in you.

I will not leave you desolate; I will come to you. Yet a little while, and the world will see me no more, but you will see me; because I live, you will live also. In that day you will know that I am in my Father, and you in me, and I in you. He who has my commandments and keeps them, he it is who loves me; and he who loves me will be loved by my Father, and I will love him and manifest myself to him.

Judas (not Iscariot) said to him:

♦ *Lord, how is it that you will manifest yourself to us, and not to the world?*

Jesus answered him:

♦ *If a man loves me, he will keep my word, and my Father will love him, and we will come to him and make our home with him. He who does not love me does not keep my words; and the word which you hear is not mine but the Father's who sent me.*

These things I have spoken to you, while I am still with you. But the Counselor, the Holy Spirit, whom the Father will send in my name, he will teach you all things, and bring to your remembrance all that I have said to you.

Peace I leave with you; my peace I give to you; not as the world gives do I give to you.

Let not your hearts be troubled, neither let them be afraid. You heard me say to you, `I go away, and I will come to you.' If you loved me, you would have rejoiced, because I go to the Father; for the Father is greater than I.

And now I have told you before it takes place, so that when it does take place, you may believe. I will no longer talk much with you, for the ruler of this world is coming. He has no power over me; but I do as the Father has commanded me, so that the world may know that I love the Father. Rise, let us go hence.

(John 14, 1 – 31; Matthew 21, 21. 22;   Mark 11, 23. 24;
 Luke 17, 6; Matthew 7, 7. 8; Luke 11, 9. 10; John 15, 7.
 16;   16, 23. 24;   15, 26;   16, 13. 14. 16;   17, 21 – 24;
 12, 49. 50; 16, 7)

The Last Time Jesus Predicts
His Great Suffering

Jesus (to his disciples):

hen I sent you out with no purse or bag or sandals, did you lack anything?

They said:

♦ *Nothing.*

He said to them:

♦ *But now, let him who has a purse take it, and likewise a bag. And let him who has no sword sell his mantle and buy one. For I tell you that this scripture must be fulfilled in me, `And he was reckoned with transgressors'; for what is written about me has its fulfilment.*

And they said:

♦ *Look, Lord, here are two swords.*

And he said to them:

91

♦ *It is enough.*

(Luke 22, 35 – 38)

Spirit of Truth Will Prove the World
Wrong and Will Glorify Jesus

Jesus (to his disciples):

have said all this to you to keep you from falling away. They will put you out of the synagogues; indeed, the hour is coming when whoever kills you will think he is offering service to God. And they will do this because they have not known the Father, nor me.

But I have said these things to you, that when their hour comes you may remember that I told you of them. I did not say these things to you from the beginning, because I was with you.

But now I am going to him who sent me; yet none of you asks me, `Where are you going?' But because I have said these things to you, sorrow has filled your hearts. Nevertheless I tell you the truth: it is to your advantage that I go away, for if I do not go away, the Counselor will not come to you; but if I go, I will send him to you. And when he comes, he will convince the world concerning sin and righteousness and judgment: concerning sin, because they do not believe in me; concerning righteousness, because I go to the Father, and you will see me no more; concerning judgment, because the ruler of this world is judged.

I have yet many things to say to you, but you cannot bear them now.

When the Spirit of truth comes, he will guide you into all the truth; for he will not speak on his own authority, but whatever he hears he will speak, and he will declare to you the things that are to come.

He will glorify me, for he will take what is mine and declare it to you. All that the Father has is mine; therefore I said that he will take what is mine and declare it to you.

A little while, and you will see me no more; again a little while, and you will see me.

Some of his disciples said to one another:

♦ *What is this that he says to us, `A little while, and you will not see me, and again a little while, and you will see me'; and, `because I go to the Father'?*

They said:

♦ *What does he mean by `a little while'? We do not know what he means.*

Jesus knew that they wanted to ask him; so he said to them:

♦ *Is this what you are asking yourselves, what I meant by saying, `A little while, and you will not see me, and again a little while, you will see me'? Truly, truly, I say to you, you will weep and lament, but the world will rejoice; you will be sorrowful, but your sorrow will turn into joy. When a woman is in travail she has sorrow, because her hour has come; but when she is delivered of the child, she no longer remembers the anguish, for joy that a child is born into the world. So you have sorrow now, but I will see you again and your hearts will rejoice, and no one will take your joy from you. In that day you will ask nothing of me.*

Truly, truly, I say to you, if you ask anything of the Father, he will give it to you in my name. Hitherto you have asked nothing in my name; ask, and you will receive, that your joy may be full.

I have said this to you in figures; the hour is coming when I shall no longer speak to you in figures but tell you plainly of the Father. In that day you will ask in my name; and I do not say to you that I shall pray the Father for you; for the Father himself loves you, because you have loved me and have believed that I came from the Father. I came from the Father and have come into the world; again, I am leaving the world and going to the Father.

His disciples said:

♦ *Ah, now you are speaking plainly, not in any figure! Now we know that you know all things, and need none to question you; by this we believe that you came from God.*

Jesus answered them:

♦ *Do you now believe? The hour is coming, indeed it has come, when you will be scattered, every man to his home, and will leave me alone; yet I am not alone, for the Father is with me. I have said this to you, that in me you may have peace. In the world you have tribulation; but be of good cheer, I have overcome the world.*

(John 16, 1 – 33;   7, 7. 33;   9, 22;   8, 29;   12, 31. 42;   13, 3. 19. 33;   14, 13. 17. 19. 21. 23. 26. 27. 29;   15, 11. 16. 19 – 21;   17, 8;   Matthew 11, 27;   26, 31;   Mark 14, 27)

Jesus Prays on Behalf of Those Who Will Believe in Him Through the Word of the Disciples

Jesus (to his disciples):

he hour is coming, indeed it has come, when you will be scattered, every man to his home, and will leave me alone; yet I am not alone, for the Father is with me. I have said this to you, that in me you may have peace. In the world you have tribulation; but be of good cheer, I have overcome the world.

When Jesus had spoken these words, he lifted up his eyes to heaven and said:

♦ *Father, the hour has come; glorify thy Son that the Son may glorify thee, since thou hast given him power over all flesh, to give eternal life to all whom thou hast given him. And this is eternal life, that they know thee the only true God, and Jesus Christ whom thou hast sent.*

I glorified thee on earth, having accomplished the work which thou gavest me to do; and now, Father, glorify thou me in thy own presence with the glory which I had with thee before the world was made.

I have manifested thy name to the men whom thou gavest me out of the world; thine they were, and thou gavest them to me, and they have kept thy word. Now they know that everything that thou hast given me is from thee; for I have given them the words which thou gavest me, and they have received them and know in truth that I came from thee; and they have believed that thou didst send me.

I am praying for them; I am not praying for the world but for those whom thou hast given me, for they are thine; all mine are thine, and thine are mine, and I am glorified in them. And now I am no more in the world, but they are in the world, and I am coming to thee.

Holy Father, keep them in thy name, which thou hast given me, that they may be one, even as we are one. While I was with them, I kept them in thy name, which thou hast given me; I have guarded them, and none of them is lost but the son of perdition, that the scripture might be fulfilled.

But now I am coming to thee; and these things I speak in the world, that they may have my joy fulfilled in themselves. I have given them thy word; and the world has hated them because they are not of the world, even as I am not of the world.

I do not pray that thou shouldst take them out of the world, but that thou shouldst keep them from the evil one. They are not of the world, even as I am not of the world. Sanctify them in the truth; thy word is truth. As thou didst send me into the world, so I have sent them into the world. And for their sake I consecrate myself, that they also may be consecrated in truth.

I do not pray for these only, but also for those who believe in me through their word, that they may all be one; even as thou, Father, art in me, and I in thee, that they also may be in us, so that the world may believe that thou hast sent me. The glory which thou hast given me I have given to them, that they may be one even as we are one, I in them and thou in me, that they may become perfectly one, so that the world may know that thou hast sent me and hast loved them even as thou hast loved me. Father, I desire that they also, whom thou hast given me, may be with me where I am, to behold my glory which thou hast given me in thy love for me before the foundation of the world.

O righteous Father, the world has not known thee, but I have known thee; and these know that thou hast sent me. I made known to them thy name, and I will make it known, that the love with which thou hast loved me may be in them, and I in them.

When Jesus had spoken these words, he went forth with his disciples across the Kidron valley, where there was a garden, which he and his disciples entered.

(John 16, 32. 33;   17, 1 – 26;   18, 1)

Jesus Prays in Gethsemane

hen Jesus went with them to a place called Gethsemane, and he said to his disciples:

♦ *Sit here, while I go yonder and pray.*

And taking with him Peter and the two sons of Zebedee, he began to be sorrowful and troubled. Then he said to them:

♦ *My soul is very sorrowful, even to death; remain here, and watch with me.*

And going a little farther he fell on his face and prayed:

♦ *My Father, if it be possible, let this cup pass from me; nevertheless, not as I will, but as thou wilt.*

And he came to the disciples and found them sleeping; and he said to Peter:

♦ *So, could you not watch with me one hour? Watch and pray that you may not enter into temptation; the spirit indeed is willing, but the flesh is weak.*

Again, for the second time, he went away and prayed:

♦ *My Father, if this cannot pass unless I drink it, thy will be done.*

And again he came and found them sleeping, for their eyes were heavy. So, leaving them again, he went away and prayed for the third time, saying the same words. Then he came to the disciples and said to them:

♦ *Are you still sleeping and taking your rest? Behold, the hour is at hand, and the Son of man is betrayed into the hands of sinners.*

Rise, let us be going; see, my betrayer is at hand.

(Matthew 26, 36 - 46;   Mark 14, 32 - 42; Luke 22, 39 - 46)

The Betrayal and Arrest of Jesus (Matthew)

hen he (Jesus) came to the disciples and said to them:

♦ *Are you still sleeping and taking your rest? Behold, the hour is at hand, and the Son of man is betrayed into the hands of sinners.Rise, let us be going; see, my betrayer is at hand.*

While he was still speaking, Judas came, one of the twelve, and with him a great crowd with swords and clubs, from the chief priests and the elders of the people. Now the betrayer had given them a sign, saying:

♦ *The one I shall kiss is the man; seize him.*

And he came up to Jesus at once and said:

♦ *Hail, Master!*

and kissed him. Jesus said to him:

♦ *Friend, why are you here?*

Then they came up and laid hands on Jesus and seized him. And behold, one of those who were with Jesus stretched out his hand and drew his sword, and struck the slave of the high priest, and cut off his ear. Then Jesus said to him:

♦ *Put your sword back into its place; for all who take the sword will perish by the sword. Do you think that I cannot appeal to my Father, and he will at once send me more than twelve legions of angels? But how then should the scriptures be fulfilled, that it must be so?*

At that hour Jesus said to the crowds:

♦ *Have you come out as against a robber, with swords and clubs to capture me? Day after day I sat in the temple teaching, and you did not seize me. But all this has taken place, that the scriptures of the prophets might be fulfilled.*

Then all the disciples forsook him and fled.

(Matthew 26, 45 - 56;   Mark 14, 41 - 51;   Luke 22, 47 - 53)

The Son of Man Will Be Seated at the Right Hand of Power, and Will Come on the Clouds of Heaven

ow the chief priests and the whole council sought false testimony against Jesus that they might put him to death, but they found none, though many false witnesses came forward. At last two came forward and said:

♦ *This fellow said, `I am able to destroy the temple of God, and to build it in three days.'*

And the high priest stood up and said:

♦ *Have you no answer to make? What is it that these men testify against you?*

But Jesus was silent. And the high priest said to him:

♦ *I adjure you by the living God, tell us if you are the Christ, the Son of God.*

Jesus said to him:

♦ *You have said so. But I tell you:*

*Hereafter you will see the Son of man
seated at the right hand of Power,
and coming on the clouds of heaven.*

Then the high priest tore his robes, and said:

♦ *He has uttered blasphemy. Why do we still need witnesses? You
have now heard his blasphemy. What is your judgment?*

They answered:

♦ *He deserves death.*

(Matthew 26, 59 - 66;   Mark 14, 55 - 64;   Luke 22, 66 - 71)

Jesus Predicts the Suffering of
the Daughters of Jerusalem

s they led him (Jesus) away, they seized one Simon of Cy-
rene, who was coming in from the country, and laid on the
cross, to carry it behind Jesus. And there followed him a
great multitude of the people, and of women who bewailed
and lamented him. But Jesus turning to them said:

♦ *Daughters of Jerusalem, do not weep for me, but weep for yourselves and for your children. For behold, the days are coming when
they will say, `Blessed are the barren, and the wombs that never
bore, and the breasts that never gave suck!' Then they will begin
to say to the mountains, `Fall on us'; and to the hills, `Cover us.'
For if they do this when the wood is green, what will happen
when it is dry?*

(Luke 23, 26 – 31)

Jesus' Promise to One of the Criminals

here was also an inscription over him: "This is the King of the Jews." One of the criminals who were hanged railed at him, saying:

♦ *Are you not the Christ? Save yourself and us!*

But the other rebuked him, saying:

♦ *Do you not fear God, since you are under the same sentence of condemnation? And we indeed justly; for we are receiving the due reward of our deeds; but this man has done nothing wrong.*

And he said:

♦ *Jesus, remember me when you come into your kingdom.*

And he said to him:

♦ *Truly, I say to you, today you will be with me in Paradise.*

(Luke 23, 38 – 43; Matthew 27, 38; Mark 15, 26. 32; John 19, 19)

The Death of Jesus (Matthew)

ow from the sixth hour there was darkness over all the land until the ninth hour. And about the ninth hour Jesus cried with a loud voice:

♦ *Eli, Eli, lema sabachthani?*

that is:

♦ *My God, my God, why hast thou forsaken me?*

And some of the bystanders hearing it said:

♦ *This man is calling Elijah.*

And one of them at once ran and took a sponge, filled it with vinegar, and put it on a reed, and gave it to him to drink. But the others said:

♦ *Wait, let us see whether Elijah will come to save him.*

And Jesus cried again with a loud voice and yielded up his spirit. And behold, the curtain of the temple was torn in two, from top to bottom; and the earth shook, and the rocks were split; the tombs also were opened, and many bodies of the saints who had fallen asleep were raised, and coming out of the tombs after his resurrection they went into the holy city and appeared to many.

When the centurion and those who were with him, keeping watch over Jesus, saw the earthquake and what took place, they were filled with awe, and said:

♦ *Truly this was the Son of God!*

There were also many women there, looking on from afar, who had followed Jesus from Galilee, ministering to him; among whom were Mary Magdalene, and Mary the mother of James and Joseph, and the mother of the sons of Zebedee.

When it was evening, there came a rich man from Arimathea, named Joseph, who also was a disciple of Jesus. He went to Pilate and asked for the body of Jesus. Then Pilate ordered it to be given to him. And Joseph took the body, and wrapped it in a clean linen shroud, and laid it in his own new tomb, which he had hewn in the rock; and he rolled a great stone to the door of the tomb, and departed. Mary Magdalene and the other Mary were there, sitting opposite the sepulchre.

Next day, that is, after the day of Preparation, the chief priests and the Pharisees gathered before Pilate and said:

♦ *Sir, we remember how that impostor said, while he was still alive, `After three days I will rise again.' Therefore order the sepulcher to be made secure until the third day, lest his disciples go and steal him away, and tell the people, `He has risen from the dead,' and the last fraud will be worse than the first.*

Pilate said to them:

♦ *You have a guard of soldiers; go, make it as secure as you can.*

So they went and made the sepulchre secure by sealing the stone and setting a guard.

(Matthew 27, 45 - 66; Mark 15, 33 - 47; Luke 23, 44 – 56)

The Death of Jesus (Luke)

t was now about the sixth hour, and there was darkness over the whole land until the ninth hour, while the sun's light failed; and the curtain of the temple was torn in two. Then Jesus, crying with a loud voice, said:

♦ *Father, into thy hands I commit my spirit!*

And having said this he breathed his last. Now when the centurion saw what had taken place, he praised God, and said:

♦ *Certainly this man was innocent.*

And all the multitudes who assembled to see the sight, when they saw what had taken place, returned home beating their breasts. And all his acquaintances and the women who had followed him from Galilee stood at a distance and saw these things.

103

Now there was a man named Joseph from the Jewish town of Arimathea. He was a member of the council, a good and righteous man, who had not consented to their purpose and deed, and he was looking for the kingdom of God. This man went to Pilate and asked for the body of Jesus. Then he took it down and wrapped it in a linen shroud, and laid him in a rockhewn tomb, where no one had ever yet been laid. It was the day of Preparation, and the sabbath was beginning. The women who had come with him from Galilee followed, and saw the tomb, and how his body was laid; then they returned, and prepared spices and ointments. On the sabbath they rested according to the commandment.

(Luke 23, 44 – 56; Matthew 27, 45 – 66; Mark 15, 33 – 47;
  John 19, 25 – 30)

7. THE RESURRECTION AND THE APPEARANCE OF OUR LORD, JESUS CHRIST

The Resurrection of Jesus and His Appearance to His Disciples (Matthew)

ow after the sabbath, toward the dawn of the first day of the week, Mary Magdalene and the other Mary went to see the sepulchre. And behold, there was a great earthquake; for an angel of the Lord descended from heaven and came and rolled back the stone, and sat upon it. His appearance was like lightning, and his raiment white as snow. And for fear of him the guards trembled and became like dead men. But the angel said to the women:

♦ *Do not be afraid; for I know that you seek Jesus who was crucified. He is not here; for he has risen, as he said. Come, see the place where he lay. Then go quickly and tell his disciples that he has risen from the dead, and behold, he is going before you to Galilee; there you will see him. Lo, I have told you.*

So they departed quickly from the tomb with fear and great joy, and ran to tell his disciples. And behold, Jesus met them and said:

♦ *Hail!*

And they came up and took hold of his feet and worshiped him. Then Jesus said to them:

♦ *Do not be afraid; go and tell my brethren to go to Galilee, and there they will see me.*

(Matthew 28, 1 - 10; Mark 16, 1 – 9; Luke 24, 1 – 7 John 20, 1 – 13)

Jesus Appears to Mary Magdalene

But Mary stood weeping outside the tomb, and as she wept she stooped to look into the tomb; and she saw two angels in white, sitting where the body of Jesus had lain, one at the head and one at the feet. They said to her:

♦ *Woman, why are you weeping?*

She said to them:

♦ *Because they have taken away my Lord, and I do not know where they have laid him.*

Saying this, she turned round and saw Jesus standing, but she did not know that it was Jesus. Jesus said to her:

♦ *Woman, why are you weeping? Whom do you seek?*

Supposing him to be the gardener, she said to him:

♦ *Sir, if you have carried him away, tell me where you have laid him, and I will take him away.*

Jesus said to her:

♦ *Mary.*

She turned and said to him in Hebrew:

♦ *Rabboni!* (which means Teacher)

Jesus said to her:

♦ *Do not hold me, for I have not yet ascended to the Father; but go to my brethren and say to them, I am ascending to my Father and your Father, to my God and your God.*

Mary Magdalene went and announced to the disciples:

♦ *I have seen the Lord;*

and she told them that he had said these things to her.

(John 20, 11 – 18)

Jesus Appears to Two Disciples
on the Road to Emmaus

hat very day two of them were going to a village named Emmaus, about seven miles from Jerusalem, and talking with each other about all these things that had happened. While they were talking and discussing together, Jesus himself drew near and went with them. But their eyes were kept from recognizing him. And he said to them:

♦ *What is this conversation which you are holding with each other as you walk?*

106

And they stood still, looking sad. Then one of them, named Cleopas, answered him:

♦ *Are you the only visitor to Jerusalem who does not know the things that have happened there in these days?*

And he said to them:

♦ *What things?*

And they said to him:

♦ *Concerning Jesus of Nazareth, who was a prophet mighty in deed and word before God and all the people, and how our chief priests and rulers delivered him up to be condemned to death, and cruci-fied him. But we had hoped that he was the one to redeem Israel. Yes, and besides all this, it is now the third day since this happened. Moreover, some women of our company amazed us. They were at the tomb early in the morning and did not find his body; and they came back saying that they had even seen a vision of angels, who said that he was alive. Some of those who were with us went to the tomb, and found it just as the women had said; but him they did not see.*

And he said to them:

♦ *O foolish men, and slow of heart to believe all that the prophets have spoken! Was it not necessary that the Christ should suffer these things and enter into his glory?*

And beginning with Moses and all the prophets, he interpreted to them in all the scriptures the things concerning himself. So they drew near to the village to which they were going. He appeared to be going further, but they constrained him, saying:

♦ *Stay with us, for it is toward evening and the day is now far spent.*

107

So he went in to stay with them. When he was at table with them, he took the bread and blessed, and broke it, and gave it to them. And their eyes were opened and they recognized him; and he vanished out of their sight. They said to each other:

♦ *Did not our hearts burn within us while he talked to us on the road, while he opened to us the scriptures?*

And they rose that same hour and returned to Jerusalem; and they found the eleven gathered together and those who were with them, who said:

♦ *The Lord has risen indeed, and has appeared to Simon!*

Then they told what had happened on the road, and how he was known to them in the breaking of the bread.

(Luke 24, 13 – 35)

Jesus Appears to His Disciples (Luke)

hen they (disciples) told what had happened on the road, and how he (Jesus) was known to them in the breaking of the bread. As they were saying this, Jesus himself stood among them, and said to them:

♦ *Peace to you.*

But they were startled and frightened, and supposed that they saw a spirit. And he said to them:

♦ *Why are you troubled, and why do questionings rise in your hearts? See my hands and my feet, that it is I myself; handle me, and see; for a spirit has not flesh and bones as you see that I have.*

108

And when he had said this, he showed them his hands and his feet. And while they still disbelieved for joy, and wondered, he said to them:

♦ *Have you anything here to eat?*

They gave him a piece of broiled fish, and he took it and ate before them. Then he said to them:

♦ *These are my words which I spoke to you, while I was still with you, that everything written about me in the law of Moses and the prophets and the psalms must be fulfilled.*

Then he opened their minds to understand the scriptures, and he said to them:

♦ *Thus it is written, that the Christ should suffer and on the third day rise from the dead, and that repentance and forgiveness of sins should be preached in his name to all nations, beginning from Jerusalem. You are witnesses of these things. And behold, I send the promise of my Father upon you; but stay in the city, until you are clothed with power from on high.*

Then he led them out as far as Bethany, and lifting up his hands he blessed them. While he blessed them, he parted from them, and was carried up into heaven.

(Luke 24, 35 – 51)

Jesus Appears to His Disciples (John)

n the evening of that day, the first day of the week, the doors being shut where the disciples were, for fear of the Jews, Jesus came and stood among them and said to them:

♦ *Peace be with you.*

When he had said this, he showed them his hands and his side. Then the disciples were glad when they saw the Lord. Jesus said to them again:

♦ *Peace be with you. As the Father has sent me, even so I send you.*

And when he had said this, he breathed on them, and said to them:

♦ *Receive the Holy Spirit. If you forgive the sins of any, they are forgiven; if you retain the sins of any, they are retained.*

(John 20, 19 – 23)

Jesus Appears to Thomas and the Other Disciples (John)

ow Thomas, one of the twelve, called the Twin, was not with them when Jesus came. So the other disciples told him:

♦ *We have seen the Lord.*

But he said to them:

♦ *Unless I see in his hands the print of the nails, and place my finger in the mark of the nails, and place my hand in his side, I will not believe.*

Eight days later, his disciples were again in the house, and Thomas was with them. The doors were shut, but Jesus came and stood among them, and said:

♦ *Peace be with you.*

110

Then he said to Thomas:

♦ *Put your finger here, and see my hands; and put out your hand, and place it in my side; do not be faithless, but believing.*

Thomas answered him:

♦ *My Lord and my God!*

Jesus said to him:

♦ *Have you believed because you have seen me? Blessed are those who have not seen and yet believe.*

(John 20, 24 – 29)

Jesus Shows Himself to His Disciples by the Sea of Tiberias (John)

fter this Jesus revealed himself again to the disciples by the Sea of Tiberias; and he revealed himself in this way. Simon Peter, Thomas called the Twin, Nathanael of Cana in Galilee, the sons of Zebedee, and two others of his disciples were together. Simon Peter said to them:

♦ *I am going fishing.*

They said to him:

♦ *We will go with you.*

They went out and got into the boat; but that night they caught nothing. Just as day was breaking, Jesus stood on the beach; yet the disciples did not know that it was Jesus. Jesus said to them:

♦ *Children, have you any fish?*

111

They answered him:

♦ *No.*

He said to them:

♦ *Cast the net on the right side of the boat, and you will find some.*

So they cast it, and now they were not able to haul it in, for the quantity of fish. That disciple whom Jesus loved said to Peter:

♦ *It is the Lord!*

When Simon Peter heard that it was the Lord, he put on his clothes, for he was stripped for work, and sprang into the sea. But the other disciples came in the boat, dragging the net full of fish, for they were not far from the land, but about a hundred yards off. When they got out on land, they saw a charcoal fire there, with fish lying on it, and bread. Jesus said to them:

♦ *Bring some of the fish that you have just caught.*

So Simon Peter went aboard and hauled the net ashore, full of large fish, a hundred and fifty-three of them; and although there were so many, the net was not torn. Jesus said to them:

♦ *Come and have breakfast.*

Now none of the disciples dared ask him:

♦ *Who are you?*

They knew it was the Lord. Jesus came and took the bread and gave it to them, and so with the fish. This was now the third time that Jesus was revealed to the disciples after he was raised from the dead.

(John 21, 1 – 14)

Jesus Reinstates Peter

hen they had finished breakfast, Jesus said to Simon Peter:

♦ *Simon son of John, do you love me more than these?*

He said to him:

♦ *Yes, Lord; you know that I love you.*

He said to him:

♦ *Feed my lambs.*

A second time he said to him:

♦ *Simon son of John, do you love me?*

He said to him:

♦ *Yes, Lord; you know that I love you.*

He said to him:

♦ *Tend my sheep.*

He said to him the third time:

♦ *Simon son of John, do you love me?*

Peter was grieved because he said to him the third time, "Do you love me?"

And he said to him:

♦ *Lord, you know everything; you know that I love you.*

Jesus said to him:

113

♦ *Feed my sheep. Truly, truly, I say to you, when you were young, you girded yourself and walked where you would; but when you are old, you will stretch out your hands, and another will gird you and carry you where you do not wish to go.*

(This he said to show by what death he was to glorify God.)

(John 21, 15 – 19)

Jesus and the Beloved Disciple

fter this (showing by what death Peter was to glorify God) he (Jesus) said to him:

♦ *Follow me.*

Peter turned and saw following them the disciple whom Jesus loved, who had lain close to his breast at the supper and had said, "Lord, who is it that is going to betray you?"

When Peter saw him, he said to Jesus:

♦ *Lord, what about this man?*

Jesus said to him:

♦ *If it is my will that he remain until I come, what is that to you? Follow me!*

The saying spread abroad among the brethren that this disciple was not to die; yet Jesus did not say to him that he was not to die, but:

♦ *If it is my will that he remain until I come, what is that to you?*

This is the disciple who is bearing witness to these things, and who has written these things; and we know that his testimony is true.

114

But there are also many other things which Jesus did; were every one of them to be written, I suppose that the world itself could not contain the books that would be written.

(John 21, 19 – 25; Matthew 16, 28)

Jesus Appears to His Disciples
for the Last Time

fterward he appeared to the eleven themselves as they sat at table; and he upbraided them for their unbelief and hardness of heart, because they had not believed those who saw him after he had risen. And he said to them:

♦ *Go into all the world and preach the gospel to the whole creation. He who believes and is baptized will be saved; but he who does not believe will be condemned. And these signs will accompany those who believe: in my name they will cast out demons; they will speak in new tongues; they will pick up serpents, and if they drink any deadly thing, it will not hurt them; they will lay their hands on the sick, and they will recover.*

So then the Lord Jesus, after he had spoken to them, was taken up into heaven, and sat down at the right hand of God. And they went forth and preached everywhere, while the Lord worked with them and confirmed the message by the signs that attended it. Amen.

(Mark 16, 14 – 20; Luke 10, 19)

8. OUR LORD, JESUS, APPEARS TO PAUL

Jesus Appears to Saul

ow as he (Saul) journeyed he approached Damascus, and suddenly a light from heaven flashed about him. And he fell to the ground and heard a voice saying to him:

♦ *Saul, Saul, why do you persecute me?*

And he said:

♦ *Who are you, Lord?*

And he said:

♦ *I am Jesus, whom you are persecuting; but rise and enter the city, and you will be told what you are to do.*

The men who were traveling with him stood speechless because they heard the voice but saw no one. Saul got up from the ground, and though his eyes were open, he could see nothing; so they led him by the hand and brought him into Damascus.

(Acts 9, 3 – 8)

Ananias Looks for a Man of Tarsus Named Saul

ow there was a disciple in Damascus named Ananias. The Lord said to him in a vision:

♦ *Ananias.*

And he said:

♦ *Here I am, Lord.*

And the Lord said to him:

♦ *Rise and go to the street called Straight, and inquire in the house of Judas for a man of Tarsus named Saul; for behold, he is praying, and he has seen a man named Ananias come in and lay his hands on him so that he might regain his sight.*

But Ananias answered:

♦ *Lord, I have heard from many about this man, how much evil he has done to thy saints at Jerusalem; and here he has authority from the chief priests to bind all who call upon thy name.*

But the Lord said to him:

♦ *Go, for he is a chosen instrument of mine to carry my name before the Gentiles and kings and the sons of Israel; for I will show him how much he must suffer for the sake of my name.*

(Acts 9, 10 – 16)

Paul in Corinth

fter this he (Paul) left Athens and went to Corinth. And he argued in the synagogue every sabbath, and persuaded Jews and Greeks. When Silas and Timothy arrived from Macedonia, Paul was occupied with preaching, testifying to the Jews that the Christ was Jesus. And when they opposed and reviled him, he shook out his garments and said to them:

♦ *Your blood be upon your heads! I am innocent. From now on I will go to the Gentiles.*

And the Lord said to Paul one night in a vision:

♦ *Do not be afraid, but speak and do not be silent; for I am with you,*

117

and no man shall attack you to harm you; for I have many people in this city.

And he stayed a year and six months, teaching the word of God among them.

(Acts 18, 1. 4 – 6, 9 – 11)

Paul Has Returned to Jerusalem

Paul (to Jews):

hen I had returned to Jerusalem and was praying in the temple, I fell into a trance and saw him saying to me:

➢ *Make haste and get quickly out of Jerusalem, because they will not accept your testimony about me.*

♦ *And I said, `Lord, they themselves know that in every synagogue I imprisoned and beat those who believed in thee. And when the blood of Stephen thy witness was shed, I also was standing by and approving, and keeping the garments of those who killed him.'*

 And he said to me:

➢ *Depart; for I will send you far away to the Gentiles.*

(Acts 22, 17 – 21)

Paul in the Barracks

hen a great clamor arose; and some of the scribes of the Pharisees' party stood up and contended:

♦ *We find nothing wrong with this man. What if a spirit or an angel has spoken to him?*

And when the dissension became violent, the tribune, afraid that Paul would be torn in pieces by them, commanded the soldiers to go down and take him by force from among them and bring him into the barracks. The following night the Lord stood by him and said:

♦ *Take courage, for as you have testified about me at Jerusalem, so you must bear witness also at Rome.*

When it was day, the Jews made a plot and bound themselves by an oath neither to eat nor drink till they had killed Paul. There were more than forty who made this conspiracy.

(Acts 23, 9 – 13)

Paul Has Testified for Jesus

Paul (to King Agrippa):

hus I journeyed to Damascus with the authority and commission of the chief priests. At midday, O king, I saw on the way a light from heaven, brighter than the sun, shining round me and those who journeyed with me. And when we had all fallen to the ground, I heard a voice saying to me in the Hebrew language:

➢ *Saul, Saul, why do you persecute me? It hurts you to kick against the goads.*

♦ *And I said, `Who are you, Lord?'*

And the Lord said:

➢ *I am Jesus whom you are persecuting. But rise and stand upon your feet; for I have appeared to you for this purpose, to appoint you to serve and bear witness to the things in which you have seen me and to those in which I will appear to you, delivering you from*

119

the people and from the Gentiles - to whom I send you to open their eyes, that they may turn from darkness to light and from the power of Satan to God, that they may receive forgiveness of sins and a place among those who are sanctified by faith in me.

(Acts 26, 12 – 18)

The Power of Jesus Is Made Perfect in Weakness

Paul (to the Corinthians):

nd to keep me from being too elated by the abundance of revelations, a thorn was given me in the flesh, a messenger of Satan, to harass me, to keep me from being too elated. Three times I besought the Lord about this, that it should leave me; but he said to me:

➢ *My grace is sufficient for you, for my power is made perfect in weakness.*

♦ *I will all the more gladly boast of my weaknesses, that the power of Christ may rest upon me.*

(2 Corinthians 12, 7 – 9)

9. OUR LORD, JESUS, APPEARS TO PETER

Jesus Appears to Peter

he next day, as they (two Cornelius' slaves and a devout soldier from the ranks of those who served him)were on their journey and coming near the city (Joppa), Peter went up on the housetop (of Simon's house) to pray, about the sixth hour. And he became hungry and desired something to eat; but

but while they were preparing it, he fell into a trance and saw the heaven opened, and something descending, like a great sheet, let down by four corners upon the earth. In it were all kinds of animals and reptiles and birds of the air. And there came a voice to him:

➢ *Rise, Peter; kill and eat.*

But Peter said:

♦ *No, Lord; for I have never eaten anything that is common or unclean.*

And the voice came to him again a second time:

➢ *What God has cleansed, you must not call common.*

This happened three times, and the thing was taken up at once to heaven.

(Acts 10, 9 – 16)

10. OUR LORD, JESUS, APPEARS TO JOHN

The Mystery of the Seven Stars and the Seven Golden Lampstands

John (the Apostle):

ehold, he is coming with the clouds, and every eye will see him, every one who pierced him; and all tribes of the earth will wail on account of him. Even so. Amen.

➢ *I am the Alpha and the Omega,*

says the Lord God,

➢ *who is and who was and who is to come, the Almighty.*

121

♦ *I John, your brother, who share with you in Jesus the tribulation and the kingdom and the patient endurance, was on the island called Patmos on account of the word of God and the testimony of Jesus. I was in the Spirit on the Lord's day, and I heard behind me a loud voice like a trumpet saying:*

➢ *Write what you see in a book and send it to the seven churches, to Ephesus and to Smyrna and to Pergamum and to Thyatira and to Sardis and to Philadelphia and to Laodicea.*

♦ *Then I turned to see the voice that was speaking to me, and on turning I saw seven golden lampstands, and in the midst of the lampstands one like a son of man, clothed with a long robe and with a golden girdle round his breast; his head and his hair were white as white wool, white as snow; his eyes were like a flame of fire, his feet were like burnished bronze, refined as in a furnace, and his voice was like the sound of many waters; in his right hand he held seven stars, from his mouth issued a sharp two-edged sword, and his face was like the sun shining in full strength. When I saw him, I fell at his feet as though dead. But he laid his right hand upon me, saying:*

➢ *Fear not, I am the first and the last, and the living one; I died, and behold I am alive for evermore, and I have the keys of Death and Hades. Now write what you see, what is and what is to take place hereafter. As for the mystery of the seven stars which you saw in my right hand, and the seven golden lampstands, the seven stars are the angels of the seven churches and the seven lampstands are the seven churches.*

(Revelation 1, 7 – 20)

122

Jesus' Message to the Angel of
the Church in Ephesus

Jesus (to John the Apostle):

o the angel of the church in Ephesus write: `The words of him who holds the seven stars in his right hand, who walks among the seven golden lampstands. `I know your works, your toil and your patient endurance, and how you cannot bear evil men but have tested those who call themselves apostles but are not, and found them to be false; I know you are enduring patiently and bearing up for my name's sake, and you have not grown weary.

But I have this against you, that you have abandoned the love you had at first. Remember then from what you have fallen, repent and do the works you did at first. If not, I will come to you and remove your lampstand from its place, unless you repent. Yet this you have, you hate the works of the Nicolaitans, which I also hate. He who has an ear, let him hear what the Spirit says to the churches. To him who conquers I will grant to eat of the tree of life, which is in the paradise of God.

(Revelation 2, 1 – 7)

Jesus' Message to the Angel of
the Church in Smyrna

Jesus (to John the Apostle):

nd to the angel of the church in Smyrna write: `The words of the first and the last, who died and came to life. `I know your tribulation and your poverty (but you are rich) and the slander of those who say that they are Jews and are not, but *are a synagogue of Satan.*

Do not fear what you are about to suffer. Behold, the devil is about to throw some of you into prison, that you may be tested, and for ten days you will have tribulation. Be faithful unto death, and I will give you the crown of life. He who has an ear, let him hear what the Spirit says to the churches. He who conquers shall not be hurt by the second death.

(Revelation 2, 8 – 11)

Jesus' Message to the Angel of the Church in Pergamum

Jesus (to John):

nd to the angel of the church in Pergamum write: `The words of him who has the sharp two-edged sword. I know where you dwell, where Satan's throne is; you hold fast my name and you did not deny my faith even in the days of Antipas my witness, my faithful one, who was killed among you, where Satan dwells.*

But I have a few things against you: you have some there who hold the teaching of Balaam, who taught Balak to put a stumbling block before the sons of Israel, that they might eat food sacrificed to idols and practice immorality. So you also have some who hold the teaching of the Nicolaitans. Repent then. If not, I will come to you soon and war against them with the sword of my mouth. He who has an ear, let him hear what the Spirit says to the churches. To him who conquers I will give some of the hidden manna, and I will give him a white stone, with a new name written on the stone which no one knows except him who receives it.

(Revelation 2, 12 – 17)

124

Jesus' Message to the Angel of
the Church in Thyatira

Jesus (to John the Apostle):

nd to the angel of the church in Thyatira write: `The words of the Son of God, who has eyes like a flame of fire, and whose feet are like burnished bronze. `I know your works, your love and faith and service and patient endurance, and that your latter works exceed the first.

But I have this against you, that you tolerate the woman Jezebel, who calls herself a prophetess and is teaching and beguiling my servants to practice immorality and to eat food sacrificed to idols. I gave her time to repent, but she refuses to repent of her immorality. Behold, I will throw her on a sickbed, and those who commit adultery with her I will throw into great tribulation, unless they repent of her doings; and I will strike her children dead. And all the churches shall know that I am he who searches mind and heart, and I will give to each of you as your works deserve.

(Revelation 2, 18 – 23)

Jesus' Message to the Believers
in Thyatira

Jesus (to John the Apostle):

ut to the rest of you in Thyatira, who do not hold this teaching, who have not learned what some call the deep things of Satan, to you I say, I do not lay upon you any other burden; only hold fast what you have, until I come. He who conquers and who keeps my works until the end, I will give him power over the nations, and he shall rule them with a rod of iron, as when earth-

en pots are broken in pieces, even as I myself have received power from my Father; and I will give him the morning star.

He who has an ear, let him hear what the Spirit says to the churches.'

(Revelation 2, 24 – 29)

Jesus' Message to the Angel of the Church in Sardis

Jesus (to John the Apostle):

nd to the angel of the church in Sardis write: `The words of him who has the seven spirits of God and the seven stars.

I know your works; you have the name of being alive, and you are dead. Awake, and strengthen what remains and is on the point of death, for I have not found your works perfect in the sight of my God.

Remember then what you received and heard; keep that, and repent. If you will not awake, I will come like a thief, and you will not know at what hour I will come upon you.

Yet you have still a few names in Sardis, people who have not soiled their garments; and they shall walk with me in white, for they are worthy.

He who conquers shall be clad thus in white garments, and I will not blot his name out of the book of life; I will confess his name before my Father and before his angels.

He who has an ear, let him hear what the Spirit says to the churches.'

(Revelation 3, 1 – 6)

126

Jesus' Message to the Angel of the Church in Philadelphia

Jesus (to John the Apostle):

nd to the angel of the church in Philadelphia write: `The words of the holy one, the true one, who has the key of David, who opens and no one shall shut, who shuts and no one opens.

I know your works.

Behold, I have set before you an open door, which no one is able to shut; I know that you have but little power, and yet you have kept my word and have not denied my name.

Behold, I will make those of the synagogue of Satan who say that they are Jews and are not, but lie - behold, I will make them come and bow down before your feet, and learn that I have loved you.

Because you have kept my word of patient endurance, I will keep you from the hour of trial which is coming on the whole world, to try those who dwell upon the earth.

I am coming soon; hold fast what you have, so that no one may seize your crown.

He who conquers, I will make him a pillar in the temple of my God; never shall he go out of it, and I will write on him the name of my God, and the name of the city of my God, the new Jerusalem which comes down from my God out of heaven, and my own new name.

He who has an ear, let him hear what the Spirit says to the churches.'

(Revelation 3, 7 – 13)

Jesus' Message to the Angel of
the Church in Laodicea

Jesus (to John the Apostle):

nd to the angel of the church in Laodicea write: `The words of the men, the faithful and true witness, the beginning of God's creation.

I know your works: you are neither cold nor hot. Would that you were cold or hot! So, because you are lukewarm, and neither cold nor hot, I will spew you out of my mouth. For you say, I am rich, I have prospered, and I need nothing; not knowing that you are wretched, pitiable, poor, blind, and naked. Therefore I counsel you to buy from me gold refined by fire, that you may be rich, and white garments to clothe you and to keep the shame of your nakedness from being seen, and salve to anoint your eyes, that you may see. Those whom I love, I reprove and chasten; so be zealous and repent. Behold, I stand at the door and knock; if any one hears my voice and opens the door, I will come in to him and eat with him, and he with me. He who conquers, I will grant him to sit with me on my throne, as I myself conquered and sat down with my Father on his throne. He who has an ear, let him hear what the Spirit says to the churches.'

(Revelation 3, 14 – 22)

Jesus Is Coming Soon

Jesus (to John the Apostle):

nd behold, I am coming soon. Blessed is he who keeps the words of the prophecy of this book.

Behold, I am coming soon, bringing my recompense, to re-

128

pay every one for what he has done. I am the Alpha and the Omega, the first and the last, the beginning and the end.

Blessed are those who wash their robes, that they may have the right to the tree of life and that they may enter the city by the gates. Outside are the dogs and sorcerers and fornicators and murderers and idolaters, and every one who loves and practices falsehood.

I Jesus have sent my angel to you with this testimony for the churches. I am the root and the offspring of David, the bright morning star.

Surely I am coming soon.

(Revelation 22, 7. 12 – 16, 20)

CONTENTS

www.ingramcontent.com/pod-product-compliance
Lightning Source LLC
Chambersburg PA
CBHW071003040426
42443CB00007B/633